CONTEMPORARY PERCUSSION

Reginald Smith Brindle, R. S.

LONDON   NEW YORK
OXFORD UNIVERSITY PRESS

Oxford University Press, Walton Street, Oxford OX2 6DP

Oxford New York Toronto
Delhi Bombay Calcutta Madras Karachi
Petaling Jaya Singapore Hong Kong Tokyo
Nairobi Dar es Salaam Cape Town
Melbourne Auckland

and associated companies in
Berlin Ibadan

Oxford is a trade mark of Oxford University Press

Published in the United States
by Oxford University Press, New York

British Library Cataloguing in Publication Data
British Library Cataloguing in Publication Data
Brindle, Reginald Smith 1917–
Contaemporary percussion.
1. Percussion instruments
I. Title
786.8
ISBN 0–19–816247–2

Library of Congress Cataloging in Publication Data

Data available

Printed in Great Britain by
Biddles Ltd, Guildford and King's Lynn

contents

acknowledgements

Extracts from the following works are reproduced by kind permission of the publishers:

Luciano Berio: *Tempi Concertati* and *Circles*; Béla Bartók: *Music for Strings, Percussion and Celesta*; Pierre Boulez: *Improvisation sur Mallarmé I/II*; Roman Haubenstock-Ramati: *Mobile for Shakespeare* and *Symphonies de Timbres*; Mauricio Kagel: *Match*; Gustav Mahler: Symphony No. 3; Olivier Messiaen: *Oiseaux Exotiques*; Karlheinz Stockhausen: *Kontakte*, *Kreuzspiel*, and *Gruppen* (Universal Edition (London) Ltd.).

Darius Milhaud: *Concerto for Percussion*; Arnold Schoenberg: *Variations for Orchestra* Op. 31; Anton Webern: *Six Pieces for Orchestra* Op. 6 (Universal Edition (Alfred A. Kalmus Ltd.)).

Gunther Schuller: *Symphony for Brass and Percussion* (Malcolm Music Ltd. (Alfred A. Kalmus Ltd.)).

Daniel Jones: *Sonata for 3 Unaccompanied Kettledrums* (© 1953 by Hinrichsen Edition Limited, London, New York, Frankfurt); Reginald Smith Brindle: *Auriga* (© 1968 by Hinrichsen Edition Limited, London, New York, Frankfurt), *Concerto for 5 Instruments and Percussion* (© 1960 by Hinrichsen Edition Limited, London, New York, Frankfurt), *Cosmos* (© 1960 by Hinrichsen Edition Limited, London, New York, Frankfurt), *Creation Epic* (© 1964 by Hinrichsen Edition Limited, London, New York, Frankfurt), *Homage to H. G. Wells* (© 1962 by Hinrichsen Edition Limited, London, New York, Frankfurt), and *Variations on a Theme of Dallapiccola* (© 1964 by Hinrichsen Edition Limited, London, New York, Frankfurt); John Cage: *Amores* (© 1943 by John Cage: © 1960 by Henmar Press Inc., New York, London, Frankfurt); Chou Wen-Chung: *All in the Spring Wind* (© 1960 by C. F. Peters Corp., New York, London, Frankfurt); Henry Cowell: *Concerto for Percussion and Orchestra* (© 1961 by C. F. Peters Corp., New York, London, Frankfurt); Ross Lee Finney: Symphony No. 2 (© 1959 by Henmar Press Inc. New York, London, Frankfurt); Alan Hovhaness: Concerto No. 8 (© 1958 by C. F. Peters Corp., New York, London, Frankfurt), Symphony No. 7 (© 1960 by C. F. Peters Corp., New York, London, Frankfurt), and Symphony No. 8 (© 1960 by C. F. Peters Corp., New York, London, Frankfurt); Toshiro

Mayuzumi: *Microcosmos* (© 1957 by C. F. Peters Corp., New York, London, Frankfurt); Robert Parris: *Concerto for Five Kettledrums* (© 1961 by C. F. Peters Corp., New York, London, Frankfurt); Heimo Erbse: *Pavimento* (© 1961 by Henry Litolff's Verlag, Frankfurt, London, New York); Milko Kelemen: *Equilibres* (© 1962 by Henry Litolff's Verlag, Frankfurt, London, New York) and *Transfigurationen* (© 1962 by Henry Litolff's Verlag, Frankfurt, London, New York); Arnold Schoenberg: *Film Music* Op. 34 (© 1930 by Heinrichshofen's Verlag, Wilhelmshaven und Amsterdam).

Béla Bartók: *Concerto for Orchestra*; Benjamin Britten: *Peter Grimes, Four Sea Interludes from Peter Grimes, War Requiem*, and *The Young Person's Guide to the Orchestra*; Aaron Copland: *Billy the Kid* and *Rodeo*; Igor Stravinsky: *Agon* and *Symphony of Psalms* (Boosey & Hawkes Music Publishers Ltd.).

Gustav Holst: *The Planets* (J. Curwen & Sons Ltd.).

William Walton: *Belshazzar's Feast* (Oxford University Press).

Claude Debussy: *Prélude à l'Après-Midi d'un Faune* (Editions Jobert, Paris).

Luigi Dallapiccola: *Variazioni per Orchestra* (Edizioni Suvini Zerboni, Milan).

Carlos Chávez: *Toccata for Percussion Instruments* (© Mills Music Inc., 1790 Broadway, New York 10019, New York, U.S.A.).

Bruno Maderna: *Concerto for Oboe*; Jean Barraqué: *Chant après Chant* (Aldo Bruzzichelli, Florence).

Edgard Varèse: *Ionisation* (© 1934 by Edgard Varèse; © 1967 by Colfranc Music Publishing Corp.; all rights reserved) and *Hyperprism* (© 1924 by Edgard Varèse; © 1966 to Colfranc Music Publishing Corp.; all rights reserved); Harold Farberman: *Concerto for Timpani & Orchestra* (© 1962 by Franco Colombo Inc.; all rights reserved).

Olivier Messiaen: *Chronochromie* (A. Leduc & Cie., 175 rue St. Honoré, Paris 1).

Joe Morello: *Sounds of the Loop* (Ludwig Drum Co., Chicago).

Paul Hindemith: *Sinfonische Metamorphosen*; Luigi Nono: *Cori di Didone* (Schott & Co. Ltd., London).

The author wishes to thank the following for their kind advice, assistance, and information during the compilation of the text of this book:

Eric Allen, James Holland, David Johnson, Jean-Charles François, Pierre Favre, Group Instrumental de Strasbourg, Christoph Caskel, Gabriel Bouchet, James Blades, Leonide Torrebruno, Aldo and Antonio Buonomo.

When *Contemporary Percussion* was first written, part of its objective was to bring to notice what was then an insufficiently exploited medium. By now, there is no longer any need for such promotion, for percussion has made itself prominent enough. Not only is it well featured in today's instrumental scores, but solo players and percussion groups have become fairly widespread, while composers, responding to a keen demand, have produced an ample solo and ensemble repertoire.

In an unforeseen way, the percussion medium seems not only to have stimulated its own growth, but has also had a considerable influence on the development of some musical styles. In some concert music and especially in various brands of popular music, the previously dominant role of melody and harmony has declined. In pop music, what was once an unobtrusive rhythmic percussion background, quietly underlining the metrical pulse, has gradually come right into the foreground, all but obliterating melody and harmony, which in any case often have no great significance. In fact, some pop music is so overpoweringly percussive 'pulse' music, that melody only rises to the surface in occasional brief fragments, while harmonic interest is slender indeed.

Percussion has also become the main protagonist in similar concert music, where again, a percussive metre is well to the fore, while melody and harmony, if present at all, have no notable role. The most significant branch of the school of minimalism is largely based on repeating percussion ostinatos which are sometimes spread over considerable periods; Steve Reich's *Drumming* has a 'free' duration of up to two hours. In minimalism, drums or mallet instruments are those most featured, as these are well suited to the musical style and the recurring, evenly flowing rhythmic patterns which form the main basis of the music. This rediscovery of rhythm in the minimalist style has achieved considerable popularity, especially with audiences which grew up with the 'beat' of pop music; but it is fairly certain that without percussion, such music could hardly have been created—certainly not in such a widely appealing fashion.

In many ways this music has much in common with African and Oriental music, particularly in the use of drums and mallet instruments playing repetitive musical formulas. Interest in such ethnic music has become intensified, so that a borrowing of influences between all the continents is common enough. If Europeans have become more aware of the music of Africa, the Orient, the Caribbean, and the Americas, there has been an equal interchange of cultures in return. Indeed Europeans could well become overshadowed in the interpretation of their own music, so powerful is the upsurge of oriental instrumental virtuosity, and this is especially so with percussionists.

It is perhaps odd that, despite ethnic influences, the percussion expansion has not brought with it a notable variety of new instruments, indeed those described in this book are still very much those in mainstream use. It is possible that this is partly the result of the Japanese takeover of instrumental production; perhaps they prefer to exploit what already exists, rather than create innovations. The only real change has been that some instruments have tended to become larger and more powerful, therefore some discretion has to be exercised in their use. For example, the large tamtams in use today may by no means produce the kind of sound and more limited volume Webern intended in 1910, while today's enormous bass drums may have astounded even Stravinsky in his younger days. However, one can safely say that in general instrumental sounds may have got louder (especially in pop music), but the general tone colours are just the same.

Ethnic instruments are now more easily available. Depending on the relative economic enterprise of native importers, a wide selection of Chinese and Indian instruments are on the market, while there is a more modest selection of instruments with African, South American, and Caribbean origins.

The only real novelties in the invention of new instruments are those of the American Harry Partch, whose creations not only produce novel wood, glass, and metal sounds, but are works of art in their own right. Partch has a fine aesthetic feeling for the visual aspect of his instruments, giving them finely sculptured, almost architectural forms, which are beautiful indeed. However, they are individual creations, perhaps too expensive and singular to spread easily into universal usage.

In the last decade the greatest development in percussion has not been strictly instrumental at all, but technological—through electronics. It is possible to synthesize a wide variety of percussion sounds, some as mere imitations of conventional instruments, others in a novel sound world where virtually any timbre and effect is possible.

In the realm of mere imitation, auto-rhythm electronic keyboards are abundantly common, in which various set-patterns are automatically played as a percussion background, while the keyboard itself is used in a conventional way, with a variety of tone colours. Other 'drum machines' or 'drum keyboards' have a double function in which, while one can play a synthesized drum set by tapping various built-in pads (each imitating a specific instrument), an auto-rhythm background can be added at will, to keep a regular pulse moving. The result can be quite complex, giving an impression of great virtuosity.

A much more ample sound world is being explored by percussionists who use a purpose-built digital mallet keyboard coupled to a computer, synthesizers, and various ancillary devices. Through the mallet keyboard, the player can create a vast array of timbres, not necessarily percussive, while other musical designs or pre-set sounds can be added through computer pre-programming and digital memory. With his mallets, the player can conjure up a vast musical panorama, the only limit being his own resourcefulness and imagination. Almost inevitably, this is the exclusive realm of the composer–performer, as he is the only person who knows the potentials of his own instrument, and no other composer or performer could create or recreate the same musical discourse.

This underlines a factor which has become abundantly evident also in conventional percussion—players with the gift of invention and spontaneous improvisation often produce virtuoso pieces which could never be conceived by composers who are not equally knowledgeable in the percussion field. Indeed, percussion instruments lend themselves to a kind of bravura playing which can hardly be put into notation, and if it were, would be extremely difficult to recreate adequately or with facility. In any case, the ideal sense of spontaneous creation could never be captured.

However, there is a danger that the resources and conveniences offered by technology can be abused. In a search for new sound worlds, and perhaps also wishing to avoid any association with conventional instrumental timbres, one can so easily introduce a distortion and harshness which is hardly musical, and is only distressing to the listener. Worse still is the temptation, through the complexities so easily generated by computer use, of creating music which is impenetrable in its complexity.

Such a work is Boulez's *Répons*, a 'dialogue' between a central group of instrumentalists, surrounded by six mallet instrument soloists. The soloist sounds are modified through the 4X computer system and then amplified. Given that the computer objective is only further to elaborate and distort the mallet instrument sounds, the result can be a mêlée of cyclonic proportions, which is hardly intelligible and highly disturbing. Such is the danger of technology misapplied.

Nevertheless, technology has its gifts, which can be musically most rewarding if used with discretion. Furthermore, for the time being at least, it offers the most fruitful avenue of exploitation and development both to the beginner and the virtuoso.

R.S.B.

August, 1990

1 | introduction

Some instruments become identified with certain musical epochs—the renaissance lutes and viols, the baroque organ, the classical string quartet, the romantic pianoforte, and so on. Our own time seems to be becoming more and more the age of percussion. In only a short span of years, percussion instruments, have come to take a dominating part in today's music. Percussion timbre is now the basis of 'contemporary sound'. Percussion players, who not long ago were regarded as the dunderheads of the orchestra, have had to step forward almost overnight and perform feats of virtuosity. The previous paucity of orchestral percussion instruments has rapidly given way to a profusion of novel instruments, some of them still in a state of evolution.

All these developments have occurred after the publication of most standard works on orchestration, where percussion has sometimes been given short shrift indeed. So this book aims at filling this partial void, providing up-to-date information on instruments, commenting on their possibilities, and occasionally trying to forecast future developments. It is addressed to the composer and arranger rather than the performer, though as the information has been gathered in several countries, many aspects of the book should also be of interest to executants whose horizons may be limited by national boundaries.

The number of percussion instruments is increasing continuously, and many of them are still in the process of development. It has not been easy to decide just what should be discussed and what excluded (for example, is the Jew's harp percussion?), and some instruments have been included which would seem to have percussion potentialities (e.g. the harpsichord) but have still hardly been used in this role.

Many opinions expressed in this book are only personal. The most expert players have often given quite conflicting views on matters which might seem beyond dispute; so the only possible procedure has been to sift information until the most commonsense solutions have emerged. For example, percussion notation is in a state of chaos: some authoritative players still regard the old stave notation as quite adequate, while others say that the sooner it is forgotten the better. The truth is that the percussion 'explosion' has happened so rapidly that players have had to fend for themselves, without the support of adequate traditions, and without the possibility, as yet, of forming a strong collective discipline.

A word about music examples. Quite a number of instruments are described without music examples being quoted. There are various reasons for this. For example, though the tablas can play quite complex music, the one or two scores which do use these highly versatile instruments contain nothing of significance. It is useless quoting examples which do not reveal the true potentialities of instruments. On the other hand, though some scores do contain parts which include what one would normally expect of certain instruments (for example, the crescendos and decrescendos of sirens in Varèse's works), to quote the music is quite superfluous. In many cases, as no short quotation from any one work can show an instrument's various possibilities, 'synthetic' examples have been written which illustrate a number of effects within a few bars.

The selection of composers whose works have been chosen for quotation may cause some raised eyebrows. Some may be virtually unknown outside their own countries. But the truth is that some of the greatest composers of this century (Schoenberg and Webern, for example) hardly used percussion at all, while much less famous contemporaries were delving into the still unassessed wealth of the percussion medium. So the names of some lesser-known composers may occur quite frequently, because they have pioneered certain usages.

One complete category of instruments has been omitted almost completely—the Orff-Schulwerk. These are very excellent instruments, but as their primary use is educational, they have been mentioned only where they can perform some useful orchestral function (usually by extending the compass of conventional instruments).

Both the history of percussion instruments and their acoustic principles are engrossing studies, but it has been felt that they are outside the scope of this book. The same is true of performing techniques. However, for those interested, books on these subjects have been included in the bibliography.

In completing this book, a thousand other lesser details have had regretfully to be suppressed for the sake of conciseness. Unfortunately, what seems less important to me may seem essential to others, so if any reader is furious because I omit such details as the fact that maracas are male and female, I beg forgiveness in advance!

2 | the classification of percussion instruments

IDIOPHONES. MEMBRANOPHONES. CHORDOPHONES. AEROPHONES.

Percussion instruments are very varied. Not only do they differ in shape and size, and in the materials used for their construction. They can also differ considerably in their acoustic principles and in the ways they are made to sound. Though most instruments are played by striking, some are shaken (e.g. maracas, sleigh bells, etc.), while others are played by scratching or scraping (e.g. the guiro). Some sound through the medium of a keyboard (e.g. celesta) and some by turning a handle (e.g. siren and rattle). Some instruments such as bird whistles even have to be blown. But they are all loosely called 'percussion'.

In a general way, however, percussion instruments may be defined as those instruments which produce sounds when struck. The resultant sounds may be anything between notes of fixed pitch and those conflicting tones we call 'noise'. They are usually divided into two separate groups, those of definite pitch and those of indefinite pitch (or, according to Forsyth's *Orchestration*, 'musical' and 'unmusical' instruments). But such a classification is rather superficial, and it is preferable to use Sachs's fourfold classification—idiophones, membranophones, chordophones, and aerophones—and then subdivide these further according to three possible musical characteristics: (1) tuned instruments, (2) instruments of indefinite pitch, (3) instruments usually considered to be of indefinite pitch but which can be tuned. *Idiophones* produce sounds through the vibration of their entire bodies, as is the case with a triangle or cymbal. In some cases there are multiple idiophones, such as the glockenspiel and tubular bells, which consist of a number of independently vibrating bodies. The sound of some idiophones is amplified by the use of resonators, as with the marimba and vibraphone, which have tuned tubular resonators fixed below each idiophone. Idiophones are usually made to sound by striking, but a number of untuned instruments are played by shaking, stroking, or scraping.

Tuned idiophones naturally emit sounds of fixed pitch, but these predominant tones are accompanied by various 'overtones' which determine the instrumental timbre. With idiophones of indefinite pitch, the overtones are so strong, profuse and conflicting, that no predominant tone is discernible. Many idiophones (e.g. the triangle, wood blocks, log drum, temple blocks, etc.), produce predominant sounds which are fairly well defined. But their sounds fuse so perfectly with any orchestral sounds and harmony that they are usually regarded as being of indefinite pitch. All instruments of indefinite pitch have of course this characteristic of blending with orchestral sounds without creating any impression of dissonance.

Membranophones produce sounds through the vibration of a membrane or skin, usually stretched tightly over a resonating tube or shell. This tube may be open at the opposite end, or it may be closed by the same material as the resonator (as is the case with timpani), or it may be closed by another membrane which vibrates in sympathy with the struck membrane. To be more exact, it is not so much a drum shell as the chamber of air it encloses which functions as a resonator.

Tuned membranophones (timpani and tablas) emit sounds of well-defined pitch. Other drums too may emit sounds of fairly fixed pitch. In fact precise tunings are sometimes indicated for tomtoms, bongos, etc. But in general drum sounds blend so well with the orchestra that they are almost universally regarded as instruments of indefinite pitch.

Chordophones produce sounds through the vibration of strings, the sound being amplified by a resonating board, box, or drum. They are all tuned instruments, and may be played by striking (cimbalom and Gascony drum) or through the medium of a keyboard (pianoforte and harpsichord).

Aerophones are instruments in which sounds are produced by causing an enclosed air column or chamber to vibrate. The vibrations are usually generated by a reed or other membrane. The reed may be an 'air reed', that is, air blown forcibly across an aperture. Sometimes there is no enclosed air chamber, the instrument itself causing the air to vibrate (e.g. the 'bull roarer').

Aerophones emit sounds of definite pitch, often of a fluctuating character (as with the siren, wind machine, bird calls etc.). But in the field of percussion only slide whistles are used as tuned instruments with a melodic role. Tuned motor horns have been scored for, but whether these can be thought of as percussion is not clear.

A further category of percussion instruments is emerging through the use of electronic techniques. For instance, contact microphones have been used to amplify the vibrations of struck surfaces, the resultant sounds being filtered and otherwise transformed to give sound effects of complete novelty. Instruments such as the electronic organ can be made to imitate existing percussion instruments, or to produce percussive sounds which are quite new and original. Further developments in this new field will certainly be seen in the near future.

3 | *notation for percussion instruments*

STAVE NOTATION. LINE-SCORE NOTATION
SYMBOL NOTATION. EXPANDED SYMBOL NOTATION

Musical notation should show the performer what he has to play in the clearest possible manner, with a minimum of signs. Furthermore, the kind of notation used should be standardized, so that a player does not have to adjust himself to a new notation for each piece of music.

Notation for tuned percussion presents no special problems. But as regards untuned percussion the situation is chaotic. There is a simple reason. No generally satisfactory notation for percussion has yet been found: solutions which are quite satisfactory for one piece of music may be quite unsuitable for another. This is especially so in *avant-garde* music. Composers use such different notations, such a proliferation of new signs and symbols, that players have to learn how to interpret the notation of each piece before they can start to play. In one score there are twenty-nine pages of music, but fifty pages of explanations as to how it is to be played! One is tempted to conclude that the novelty of these pieces may sometimes be not so much in the music itself as in the way it is written.

Some systems do point towards a standard notation which, if universally accepted, would satisfy the criteria of clarity, economy, and uniformity. But before considering ideal solutions, it is preferable to examine the three main kinds of notation already in use, so that their advantages and defects may be appreciated.

Stave Notation
In the past, percussion notation has frequently used the conventional five-line stave coupled usually with the bass clef. This has been very suitable where the instruments are 'standard' and few in number. Perhaps its most successful application has been in the field of jazz. A jazz 'set' is much the same all the world over, and drummers are accustomed to a notation which uses the five-line stave and the bass clef. The instruments most often used—bass drum and snare drum—are usually indicated by ordinary notation in the first and third

spaces (A and E in the bass clef). The suspended ('ride') cymbal is shown as
an asterisk in the top space (G), while the foot cymbals ('high hat'), if indicated
at all, are inserted as an asterisk in the second space (C). (However, 'high hat'
cymbals are so invariably used for an 'off-beat' rhythm that indications are
omitted, except for some special effect.)

These instruments are basic for a jazz outfit, but the inclusion of two
tomtoms and crash cymbal has become almost standard. The two tomtoms
are indicated in the second and fourth spaces (C and G) in ordinary notation,
while the crash or 'sizzle' cymbal is shown in the same way as the 'ride'
cymbal, but with a circle round the asterisk. (Sometimes the tomtom notes
are circled, though there seems no real need for this.)

The following is therefore a notation which should be readily understood
by all jazz drummers:

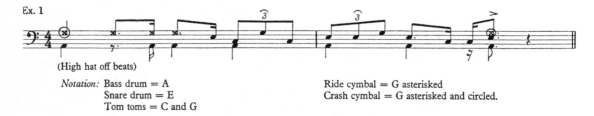

Ex. 1

(High hat off beats)

Notation: Bass drum = A   Ride cymbal = G asterisked
           Snare drum = E   Crash cymbal = G asterisked and circled.
           Tom toms = C and G

Jazz notation avoids placing notes on the lines except when there is no
room to put a note in its usual place. In fact, bass drum and cymbal notes are
often displaced in a haphazard way to make room for other parts. It therefore
usually places notes only in the four spaces, and obviously this causes the
system to be very restricted. The more exotic jazz instruments (maracas,
claves, congas, etc.) have no specific notation and are usually shown in the
same space as the snare drum (E). If jazz notation did include notes on the
lines and above and below the stave, indications could be made standard for
twelve different instruments (if we include the asterisk for cymbals) and the
notation would be clear, efficient, and virtually complete for all but exceptional
purposes.

In concert music untuned percussion notation has been written on the
conventional five-line stave for almost two hundred years, but nothing has
become standard. No single note is universally accepted as indicating a
specific instrument. Some composers show all notation in the treble clef,
others in the bass clef, others use only the C clef. Others, again, perhaps in a
misguided attempt at representing the big diversity of pitch in untuned percussion instruments, use two or three clefs. Of course, the result is unsatis-
factory. The following is an example taken from one of the author's own
scores which used notation recommended in an orchestration book:

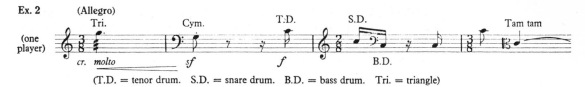

(T.D. = tenor drum.   S.D. = snare drum.   B.D. = bass drum.   Tri. = triangle)

The result is quite obscure. The player has to read an excessive number of symbols, while the use of the five-line stave and clefs carries implications of pitch which bear no relation to the real sounds. If a few more instruments had been added, the part would have been almost undecipherable.

On reading through scores which use the five-line stave for untuned percussion, it is remarkable what diverse notation is given for even the most common instruments. There is absolutely no uniformity of usage. It is also remarkable how the third space is used so much more than any other, to indicate the most varied instruments. In many cases, composers use a separate stave for each instrument, so that a large space in the score is occupied by only a few instruments. Sometimes too each instrumental part is copied separately, necessitating a large number of percussion players for only a moderate number of instruments. Yet the parts are often so elementary that one player alone could play all the instruments, if only he had a satisfactory notation.

There would be some advantage in retaining the five-line stave if each space and line invariably indicated a specific instrument. But this is certainly not the case now, and probably never will be. Even if each line and space were always to indicate the same instrument, the stave can only show eleven instruments, which is often inadequate.

The use of the conventional five-line stave is therefore not satisfactory. It is too limited in its possibilities, it implies pitch relationships which are quite unreal, and it is unsuitable for indicating the passage-work over a wide variety of instruments which is such a prominent feature in many modern scores.

Line-Score Notation

A much more satisfactory notation, adopted early in this century, indicates the part of each individual instrument on a separate line. This notation has its defects, but it avoids the pitch-implications of the stave, while showing each individual part with the utmost clarity:

Ex. 3

(One performer)

If the instruments can be positioned for playing so as to correspond to their ordering in the score, the player's task is greatly eased. For instance, in the above example, instruments can be positioned from right to left, beginning with the top line downwards (i.e. cymbal, snare drum, bass drum, tamtam).

Where it is possible to place instruments on the bottom line near the player, and those on upper lines progressively further away (as in Ex. 6.), we have a one-to-one relationship between notation and instrumental positioning. Such correspondences between instrumental positioning and notation should always be sought for, though they are only possible when a few instruments are used.

There are two main disadvantages in this notation. Firstly, the player has to observe the rests shown on every line in order to work out the correct rhythmic configuration of the music. Secondly, with only one instrument on each line, he cannot read many lines at once and so can play only a few instruments. It is to be observed that in *Ionisation* by Varèse, a pioneer of this system of notation, none of the thirteen percussion players is given more than five lines to read, in fact only two performers have more than three lines. With a more economical notation *Ionisation* could be played just as well by fewer performers.

As a variant of line-score notation, some composers write for all percussion instruments on one line only. In this case the previous example would appear as follows:

Ex. 4

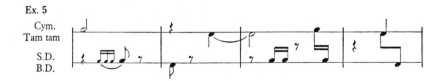

This method has the advantage of showing the rhythmic design with great clarity, but unfortunately every instrument has to be indicated by an abbreviation—inconvenient for the player in whose language the abbreviated words occur, but much more so for a foreigner. (This problem can be easily solved by using graphic symbols for each instrument, but it is best to defer discussion of this till later.)

Perhaps the most suitable notation for the previous two examples would be as follows:

Ex. 5

By using two lines, and notating instruments either above or below each line, each instrumental part is perfectly clear. Placed in a suitable position, a single 'set' of rest signs indicates the rhythmic design with maximum clarity and economy. The connection of the stems of quaver and semiquaver notes, even when these are for different instruments, further contributes to the clarity of the rhythmic figuration.

It would be possible to write for more instruments with this notation by using notes *on* the lines as well as above and below. But perhaps this usage is best reserved for those special cases where there are three or more of one kind of instrument—for example three wood blocks, three tomtoms, five temple blocks, etc. In this case, notes could be written on, above, and below the lines as follows:

Ex. 6
3 wood blocks
5 temple blocks
3 tom toms

As will be seen, this method of notation permits the writing of quite complex music for all eleven instruments with the utmost clarity. No other solution seems practical.[1]

There is another matter which needs consideration if a standard notation is to be achieved. This is the vertical ordering of instruments. Even when parts are clearly arranged as in the previous two examples, performers can never be sure what vertical ordering of instruments to expect. For instance, in one piece of music the drums may be on lines above the cymbals, in the next below, and so on. It would be of great assistance to percussionists if instruments were always scored in the *same vertical order*. I would like to suggest that metal instruments should always be above, wood next below, and membranes at the bottom. Tuned percussion could be placed between the wood and membranes, and the timpani below the other membranes. Within each group ('metal', 'wood', and 'membranes'), higher pitched instruments should be above those of lower pitch.

The vertical order of instruments in a line-score should then appear as

[1] It is worth noting, however, that some composers who have pioneered line-score notation (such as Stockhausen) never write notes both on, and above and below the lines. Notes are shown only on separate lines or in separate spaces, never both (as in Exx. 90 and 183), and it must be admitted that the resulting notation is very clear indeed. The one disadvantage is that many more lines are required. For instance, Ex. 6 would need eleven lines instead of only four. This 'on-the-lines-only' notation could be used when only a few instruments are scored for, but once adopted it must be adhered to throughout a score, otherwise confusion will result.

follows, though no single player's part will normally include so many instruments:

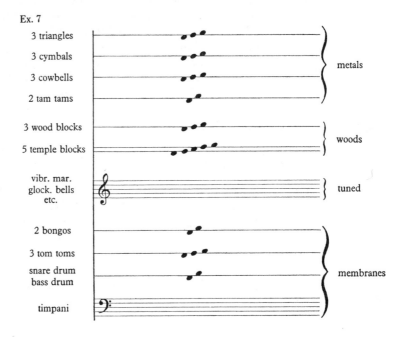

Ex. 7

The instruments in this example include only the more conventional ones. Other more exotic instruments could be included in their appropriate sections (according to whether they are 'metal', 'wood', or 'membranes'). Naturally, there is little music which requires such a vast array of instruments to be played by one performer, but a handful of such pieces does already exist, and in the future, it is likely that there will be many more. But even if a player has only to use a few instruments, it is recommended that they be laid out in his part in the above order, naturally omitting lines for those instruments which are not used. The only exception to this ordering should be when a part is written throughout for only a few instruments, and their position in the score corresponds to the most suitable placing of the instruments in performance (i.e. instruments nearest the player are shown in the bottom line and those on the upper lines are placed progressively further away).

It is certain that performers can already deal with much more demanding percussion parts than those they usually have to play now. And as a single performer can play a fairly large number of instruments with much greater rhythmic precision than could several players using the same instruments, everything points towards the concentration of percussion work into the hands of one or two good players, rather than the dispersal of music among several possibly more mediocre performers. Hence the need to standardize a notation which, like line-score notation, is suitable for use with a large number of instruments.

It must again be stressed that a line-score should be kept as simple as possible. A large line-score can be very difficult to read, not only because it covers such a big area, but also because many horizontal lines, spotted here and there with notes, form visual patterns which are not easily deciphered. In a part for 'multiple' percussion, it is thus wise not to have horizontal lines for instruments (or instrumental groups) which are not in use.

Symbol Notation

The possibility has already been mentioned of using graphic symbols for each instrument. This recently evolved method enables the performer to see immediately which instrument is to be used, and has the great advantage of allowing the composer to write for almost all instruments on only one or two lines. The rhythmic configuration of the music is shown with absolute clarity, and there is no doubt that parts written with this notation are much more economical in space and are far easier to read, than any of the methods previously mentioned.

As an illustration, if the four symbols ⌣ ◩ ☐ and △ represent suspended cymbal, snare drum, tomtom, and triangle, music for these four instruments can be written on one line as follows:

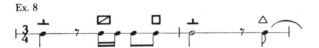

Ex. 8

For more complex music, two lines are necessary if there are rapid passages from one instrument to another. In the following example, three each of tom-toms (☐), temple blocks (⊖) and wood blocks (▬) are used, as well as snare drum and cymbal, and notes are written on, above and below the lines, to show which instrument is to be played in each group of three:

Ex. 9

This method of notation seems to have many advantages and few defects.

The parts are perfectly clear, economical in space, and readily comprehensible to performers of all nationalities. The most obvious defect seems to be that if only two lines are used, it may not always be possible to keep the same instruments on the same lines. In the previous example the snare drum and tomtoms have both changed lines towards the end, and this could easily lead to confusion and mistakes. This defect could be largely avoided by using more lines, so that instruments are always written on the same line. But of course if this is carried too far, 'symbol' notation becomes virtually 'line-score' notation, covers too large an area, and loses legibility. It is best to keep the number of lines used in any musical section down to the minimum necessary for a clear and unambiguous indication of the music.

A number of symbols are already in use and these can be augmented to cover a considerable range of instruments, as follows:

Metals

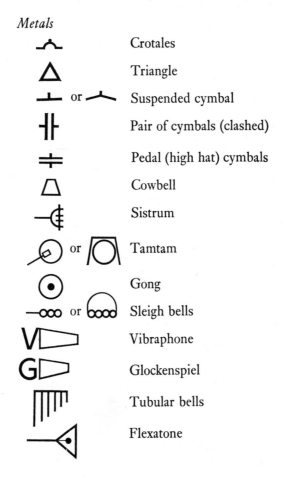

Crotales

Triangle

Suspended cymbal

Pair of cymbals (clashed)

Pedal (high hat) cymbals

Cowbell

Sistrum

Tamtam

Gong

Sleigh bells

Vibraphone

Glockenspiel

Tubular bells

Flexatone

Woods

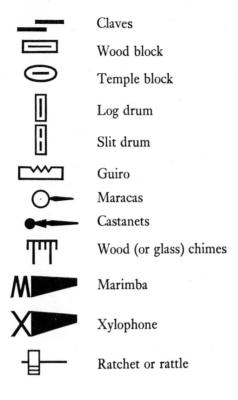

Claves

Wood block

Temple block

Log drum

Slit drum

Guiro

Maracas

Castanets

Wood (or glass) chimes

Marimba

Xylophone

Ratchet or rattle

Membranes

Bongos

Tambourine

Timbales

Tomtom

Wooden-headed tomtoms

Snare drum with snare

Snare drum without snare

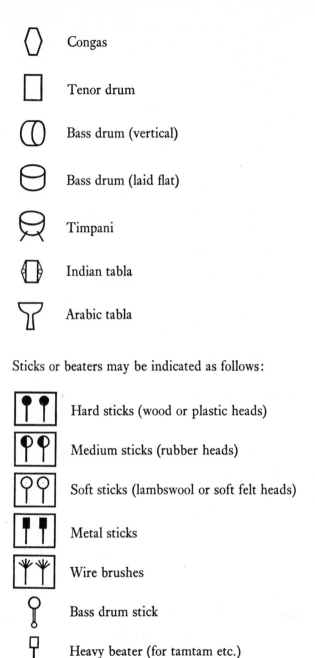

Congas

Tenor drum

Bass drum (vertical)

Bass drum (laid flat)

Timpani

Indian tabla

Arabic tabla

Sticks or beaters may be indicated as follows:

Hard sticks (wood or plastic heads)

Medium sticks (rubber heads)

Soft sticks (lambswool or soft felt heads)

Metal sticks

Wire brushes

Bass drum stick

Heavy beater (for tamtam etc.)

It is also possible to show two sticks in each hand, which may be of the same kind, or with different degrees of hardness:

 two hard sticks in each hand

 two soft sticks (l.h.) and two hard sticks (r.h.)

Finally, to indicate notes played at the centre of an instrument (if this is unusual, as on the timpani or cymbal) notes may be ringed thus: ⊘ . Sounds played at or near the rim can have a triangular form and are better written as 'white' notes for easier identification: ⊽ . A return to the normal beating spot is indicated merely by the resumption of normal notation. The above notation is particularly necessary where there are rapid changes of beating spot and there is no room to write the usual indications such as 'at the centre', 'at the rim', etc.

The above list of symbols is fairly comprehensive. It does not include symbols for the more exotic instruments, but these in any case do not lend themselves to readily comprehensible graphic designs.

Apart from line-score and symbol notations, no other system of percussion notation seems to have emerged which is clear, economical, and readily comprehensible. If one had to choose between the two, the simplicity, economy, and clarity of symbol notation would seem to make it an obvious first choice. Nevertheless, line-score notation cannot be abandoned easily. Many passages come to mind which cannot be written in symbol notation. For instance, the following passage from Berio's *Tempi Concertati* shows rapid passage-work over a number of instruments which lends itself well to the line-score, but could hardly have been written in any other way.

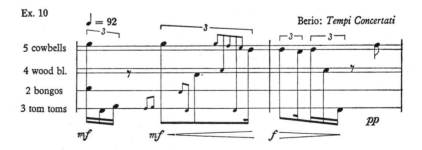

Ex. 10   Berio: *Tempi Concertati*

Symbol notation would in fact create grave obstacles to the player.

However it should be possible not to opt for one or other notation, but to fuse them together into one efficient system which could become standard in all percussion parts. This would use symbol notation as a basis, and expand this towards the line-score only where clarity makes this essential. The following is an example of an *expanded symbol notation*. It covers a big array of different instruments, yet all the information the player needs is kept within a small area:

Ex. 11

This example includes sounds from twenty-two instruments. In line-score eight lines and two staves would have been necessary for this music, but in expanded symbol notation, three lines and one stave are the most that are needed, and that at only one point. As this example includes more instruments than one player can be fairly expected to handle within the space of six bars, it seems probable that this notation is sufficient for all but the most exceptional circumstances.

In addition to its being so easy to read, this form of notation is also very simple to write. There are virtually only two criteria to be observed: (1) the music should be written on as few lines as clarity allows, and (2) the vertical ordering of instruments (when two or more lines are used) should always be according to the standard laid down for line notation.

To sum up, symbol notation is the most suitable general notation. In simple situations, only one line need be used. Where the music must indicate a variety of instruments in rapid succession, expanded symbol notation should be used, employing as few lines as clarity permits. The line-score method should be reserved for those situations where it becomes the most legible notation for indicating rapid passage-work over a variety of instruments. But even when the line-score is used, this should be merged into the symbol notation which will prevail in much of the score, thus creating one comprehensive system of notation readily understood by all players.

At all times, clarity, economy, and simplicity should be our chief criteria. Above all, we should never depart from orthodoxy for the sake of novelty. It is easy to yield to the temptation of creating a new notation, just for the pleasure of making something new and strange, but there is no guarantee that every player will have the patience to read it.

4 | percussion layouts and the placing of instruments

THE PLACING OF INSTRUMENTS

THE NUMBER OF PLAYERS REQUIRED

The Placing of Instruments

Not infrequently one sees players looking over their shoulders to see the conductor, carrying sheets of music from one place to another, struggling round the back of the tubular bells to get at the bass drum, and so on. These inconveniences could all be avoided by a little thought and planning on the composer's part. If the instruments are already 'positioned' in the composer's mind when he writes the music, and the plan of this positioning is given to the player by being reproduced in the score and parts, the performer's 'work-movement' problems are solved. Stravinsky did this as long ago as *Histoire du Soldat*, and incidentally, by evolving an original instrumental layout, wrote some ingenious percussion music which could hardly be played in any other way.

There are three main aspects to be considered:

(1) *Distance*. Instruments must be disposed so that the player has a minimum distance to move from one instrument or instrumental group to another.

(2) *Direction*. Players should not have to turn their backs on the conductor while moving to an instrument or playing it.

(3) *Reading music*. It is impossible for the player to read from one music stand if he has to move about a lot. He should be able to see the music and the conductor in the same glance, so when necessary he should have more than one set of parts disposed on stands in various positions.

Naturally these remarks only apply to situations where a performer (or each player of a group) has to play a fair number of instruments. Otherwise problems are easily solved by the players themselves.

The following illustration (Fig. 1) is an example of the excellent planning of multiple percussion in the score of Berio's *Circles*. This is a plan of the instrumental layout for the second percussionist. To see the singer and two

Fig. 1.

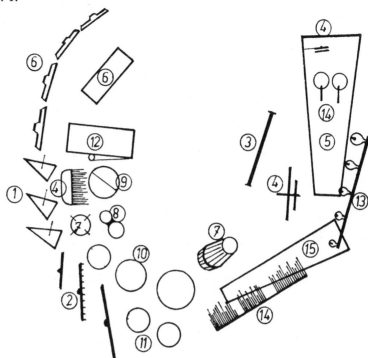

KEY

1. 3 triangles
2. 3 suspended cymbals (the medium with sizzles)
3. Tamtam
4. Hi-hat cymbals, also glass chimes and clap cymbals
5. Vibraphone
6. 4 chinese gongs, also glockenspiel
7. Tambourine and 1 tabla
8. 2 bongos
9. Snare drum
10. 3 tomtoms
11. 2 congas
12. Bass drum with footpedal
13. 5 temple blocks
14. Maracas, also wood chimes
15. Xylophone

(Some numbers are duplicated. This is because some lines in the score are used for several instruments, the score being laid out from top to bottom in the above order.)

other players, the performer has to look to the bottom left, so that except when playing the vibraphone, he always has the other players in view. Only the tamtam seems inconveniently placed, where it can be knocked over by any false move.

It must be remembered that it is not sufficient for an instrument to be just within reach. The player must be able to put himself in a satisfactory playing position. Some instruments need to be played with a certain stance, others need to be struck forcibly from a certain angle, and so on. So do not expect a player to be happy about playing the marimba over the top of the timps, or striking the tamtam while leaning over backwards.

The Number of Players Required

In theory, a composer should decide how many percussion players he is going to use before he begins to write. But this is not always easy. Often enough a decision can only be made after the music has been written, in which case the percussion parts will have to be re-written for whatever number of players is necessary. However, when a composer does wish to decide how many players he will need, there are several issues to be considered. It is not only a question of the number of notes or number of instruments to be played.

More than one player is necessary in three circumstances:

(1) When several instruments have to be played together or in quick succession with a force which is beyond the physical possibilities of one player.

(2) When there are complex rhythmic patternings on a number of instruments. For instance, an overlay of rhythmic patterns on different instruments, each quite simple in itself, may produce a total result of some complexity.

(3) When a number of instruments have to be played simultaneously, or in such quick succession that one player could not reach them. This is particularly the case when large instruments are in use such as the marimba, timpani, and tubular bells.

It is preferable to use only one player when none of the above factors prevents this, for the following reasons:

Economy. A piece is more likely to be performed if it is economical in means (other things being equal!). In addition, if only one player is asked for, he is more likely to be the best available.

Precision. One player can play rapid successions of notes on a number of instruments with greater precision than when the instruments are played by two or more performers.

Style. A single player will obviously play with a consistent, uniform style. A number of players may not do so.

Parts may sometimes be written for a 'minimum' number of players. When large orchestras have more percussion players than are needed, the extra players often take over certain instruments, especially those which are large and need to be played with force. So it is possible to write for a small number of players, with an eye to economy, knowing that in large orchestras more performers will probably be used.

5 | *factors influencing timbre*

THE ACOUSTIC PRINCIPLE OF IDIOPHONES
THE ACOUSTIC PRINCIPLE OF MEMBRANOPHONES
THE TONAL IMPORTANCE OF BEATERS
THE INFLUENCE OF THE BEATING SPOT ON TIMBRE
CONTACT SOUNDS. FINGER-STYLE PLAYING

In the following chapters there will be frequent references as to how the timbre of each instrument may be altered. But the principles are so much the same—depending on similar acoustic phenomena—that it is best to summarize these first. The following remarks only apply to instruments which are struck, as the timbre of those instruments which are shaken, stroked, or scraped cannot be modified.

The Acoustic Principle of Idiophones
Though idiophones are so varied in shape and size, the basic acoustic principles are common to all of them. These phenomena can best be illustrated by discussing the vibrations which occur in a simple metal bar, such as a vibraphone key.

When struck, the bar can vibrate in various ways. It can vibrate along the whole of its length, to produce its lowest (fundamental) sound. At the same time it can also vibrate in aliquot parts, that is, in halves, thirds, quarters, fifths, sixths, and so on. These shorter vibrations produce harmonics or 'overtones'. In fact, the bar can vibrate in quite small fractions of its total length, to produce very high overtones indeed. Whole length, half length and one-third length vibrations of a flat surface (such as a metal bar) may be illustrated as follows:

Fig. 2.

Overtones may be almost inaudible (as with the vibraphone), or very strong indeed (as with cymbals and tamtams), and it is their number and strength which establish the timbre of sound.

The acoustic principle of membranophones

A membranophone consists of a skin stretched over a hollow resonating chamber. Though membranes vibrate in a complex way (drum skins vibrate in both circular and segmental patterns), it is sufficient for our purposes to say that a membrane vibrates across its radius in whole parts, in halves, thirds, quarters, etc. to produce a fundamental tone and various harmonic overtones. As with idiophones, the number and strength of these overtones affects the timbre of the instrument.

One essential part of membranophones cannot be altered—the resonator. This not only amplifies the vibration of the membrane, but strengthens certain tones. This means that these tones will always tend to predominate, however the membrane is struck.

The tonal importance of beaters

The timbre and apparent pitch of both idiophones and membranophones can vary considerably according to the type of beater used. In general they affect timbre through two factors: (1) the degree of hardness or softness of the beater head, and (2) the contact area of the beater. When a soft beater strikes an instrument, its head 'gives', spreading momentarily, but just long enough to impede vibrations of short wavelength. High overtones are therefore smothered before they have a chance to sound, so that only the fundamental and lower harmonics are heard. This gives mellow, deep timbres. Beaters with hard heads have less give, or even virtually none at all. Thus high overtones are not impeded and the sound is 'bright'.

If a beater has a large contact area, again high overtones are prevented. On the other hand, a beater with a very small contact area (e.g. a thin, hard rod) will elicit high overtones to a marked degree, and possibly leave lower sounds almost inaudible. (Soft beaters tend to have large contact areas, hard beaters small, so these two factors normally reinforce each other.)

The combined effects of large or small contact areas and soft or hard beater heads may be roughly illustrated as Fig. 3.

Some instruments alter their timbre (and even their apparent pitch) much more than others, with the kind of beater used. For instance, a tamtam can be made to produce completely contrasting sounds with a very soft beater and a very hard beater. Again, if a cymbal is struck at the rim with something broad and soft (like the foam-rubber sole of a slipper), all overtone vibrations are eliminated by the soft, broad area of contact, and the instrument has a pure, deep gong-like sound. If the same instrument is struck at the same spot, and with the same force, but with a thin metal rod, only the highest overtones are

Fig. 3.

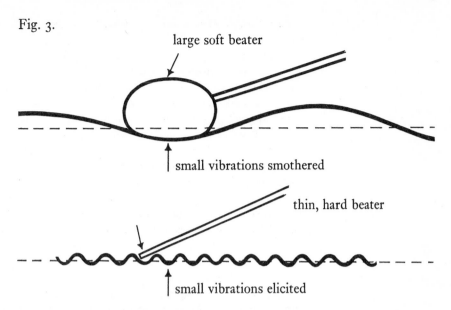

large soft beater

small vibrations smothered

thin, hard beater

small vibrations elicited

elicited, and the sound is shrill and piercing. But whatever beater is used on a marimba, though the sound may be deep or bright, mellow or hard, and may seem to be in one octave or another, the *tone* will always be that of a marimba.

The influence of the beating spot on timbre

In general, if idiophones and membranophones are struck at or near the edge, high overtones will be elicited, if at or near the centre, deeper tones will predominate. The timbre will accordingly be bright or dull, harsh or mellow, and the pitch may be apparently high or low. But this can only be a rough generalization. Some instruments are impeded from vibrating at the centre, others at the edge. Some are shaped so that only certain areas vibrate freely. In such cases, it can be said that at or near restricted edges or areas, higher sounds will be produced (and therefore brighter timbre) than in the middle of freely vibrating areas.

Some instruments have a special point which produces the most characteristic timbre (usually a combination of both high and low tones). This is the conventional 'beating spot', and timbre may be modified by changing the position of the beating spot to areas which will produce brighter or darker tone colours.

Contact Sounds

In addition to the normal sounds produced by the vibrations of an instrument, there is a 'contact' sound produced by the impact of one surface against another.

Contact sounds are most prominent when two hard surfaces strike each other, whereas with soft surfaces, or when one surface is soft, there is virtually no contact sound at all. Its presence or absence can greatly influence the musical quality and suitability of an instrument's sound. If for instance, a vibraphone is played with very soft beaters, there is almost no contact sound, and the bars respond with their normal full tones. If, however, the instrument were to be played (by some freak of fortune) with the cane ends of vibraphone beaters, there would be a fair rattle of contact sounds, but the bars would respond with only very feeble tones.

Contact sounds are not normally desired, and are usually suppressed to some degree. Nevertheless, they are perfectly apt in some musical situations, especially where a bright, hard edge to the tone is desirable.

Finger-style playing

It should be borne in mind that most struck percussion instruments can also be played with the fingers, knuckles, fingernails, or flat of the hands. Such 'finger-style' playing is by no means common, but the quiet sonorities and variety of timbres which can be obtained make this style of playing ideally suited to chamber music, and in the future it is certain to become more developed. Finger playing is discussed later with reference to drums, but it should be cultivated for all struck instruments.

6 | *writing for keyboard percussion*

GENERAL. HAMMERINGS. DOUBLE BEATS. CROSS-OVER BEATS

THE TREMOLO. CHORDS OF THREE OR MORE NOTES. GLISSANDOS

ALEATORY INDICATIONS. OCTAVE TRANSPOSITIONS

Tuned percussion instruments of the xylophone family have established a leading position among percussion instruments because of their dual (melodic and colouristic) character.

Composers have seized on these instruments with particular enthusiasm during the present period of radical stylistic transformation and search for new means of expression. For they can effectively produce a new sound panorama (quite different from 'classical' orchestral sound) which suits the ethos of contemporary musical expression.

In the last decade the music written for tuned percussion instruments has developed with unprecedented rapidity, and the technical demands have become more and more complex almost from day to day. If the present rate of development is continued, we will soon reach the stage when composers may believe that 'everything is possible'. But not everything is possible. Though players have responded wonderfully to composers' demands, their protests are rightly often violent. Their chief complaint is that composers do not understand the instruments well enough. Often a certain passage is not only difficult but decidedly risky, just because of one small detail; a simple octave displacement of one note or the substitution of another can transform an infuriatingly difficult passage into something which comes off with brilliance.

This, then is the important point. To write well for any instrument, we must write music which can be played with comparative ease and therefore brilliance. However complex the passage may be, it should fit 'under the beaters', so that it can be played with a flourish. But this can never be done if the performer has to tie his arms in knots with rapid successions of cross-over beats, interspersed with leaps from one end of the instrument to the other.

Such difficulties also endanger the rhythmic flow. This is particularly

evident with the xylophone, since the clear, precise sound of the instrument
reveals every rhythmic flaw. We have all heard xylophone passages which
'stagger'. The fault is often not the player's but the composer's. The author
was once dissatisfied because a certain xylophone passage in one of his works
was never played with enough rhythmic verve and precision. Now he knows
better—there are too many awkward corners in the music for it ever to come
off well.

It is therefore necessary for composers to imagine how their music will be
played, to foresee what difficulties will arise, and if possible to eliminate them.
Then their music can come off brilliantly. Notice how Messiaen has thought
out his virtuoso keyed percussion parts so thoroughly in *Chronochromie* that
he includes hammering indications.

The following section deals with difficulties in keyboard percussion playing. However, it must be stressed that performers are technically prepared to
overcome most problems with comparative ease, so there is no need to write
music completely void of pitfalls. The main point of these remarks is to dis-
courage music which is ridiculously difficult or impossible.

The chief problem players have to contend with is the sheer size of some
of their instruments, and the different spacing of keys between one instrument and another. For instance, a marimba is almost seven feet (2.2 m.) long,
and one octave can span 20 in. (52 cm.). On the other hand a glockenspiel
is little over two feet (62 cm.) long and an octave spans 10 in. (26 cm.) or less.
Obviously, music can be written which passes from one end of the glockenspiel to the other with extreme rapidity, but this must be avoided with the
marimba.

Players are trained to look at their keyboard as little as possible (so as to
keep one eye on their music and the other on the conductor). This is all very
well if a performer always plays a single instrument. But if (like most players)
he has to make a living by playing the vibraphone, xylophone, marimba, or
glockenspiel at short notice, he is faced with instruments not only of different
sizes, but with different keyboard layouts. For instance, the two layers of
bars (natural notes near the player, sharps and flats in the rear) are level on
the vibraphone and occasional xylophones, but on other instruments the rear
layer is higher and projects over the front bars. In addition, the bars are wider
on some instruments than on others so that the spacing between any two
notes is not the same. To add to this difficulty, all bars on the xylophone,
glockenspiel, and most vibraphones are usually of equal width, so that the
span between notes in different octaves is the same. But marimbas and some
vibraphones have wide bars in the low register, which graduate to narrower
bars in the high register, so that intervals in different octaves have a different
span.

These are problems which concern the player rather than the composer.

But the practical outcome is that performers often have to memorize difficult passages to make sure they make no mistakes. Given the limited rehearsal time usually allotted to modern works, this is not always possible.

Hammerings

The worst difficulties a performer has to face, and which can be eliminated if the composer or orchestrator has a little foresight, concern hammerings, that is, the way the keys are beaten. The major problems usually occur only in rapid passages, and involve:

(1) situations in which notes are wide apart and cannot be played 'hand to hand';
(2) passages which require inconvenient 'double beats';
(3) awkward cross-hammerings.

Wherever possible rapid music written for keyed percussion should be such that it can be played 'hand to hand' with alternate hammers and without cross-over beats (particularly when this entails moving on to the rear row of keys and back again):

Ex. 12

Messiaen: *Oiseaux Exotiques*

In this passage, played throughout with alternate hammers, there are no cross-over beats, and Messiaen spreads the notes out gradually over a wide area in the final bar in such a way that the leaps are gradual and easily accomplished.

The same hand-to-hand technique, without cross-over beats, allows the following passage to be played extremely rapidly in spite of the large leaps which occur:

Ex. 13

Boulez: *Une Dentelle s'Abolit*

However, such straightforward beating must sometimes be abandoned and double beats and cross-overs resorted to.

Double beats (two consecutive strokes with the same hammer) can be quite effective in some circumstances. For instance, where they can be made to fit into a repeated pattern, a player can preform double beats with ease and precision:

Here the musical design is clear, and coincides with the double-beat pattern so closely that the performer is not presented with a difficult mental exercise and can concentrate on the physical problems. But double beats cannot always be set in such symmetrical patterns, and more often they occur in such a haphazard way as to create obstacles to the smooth flow of the music:

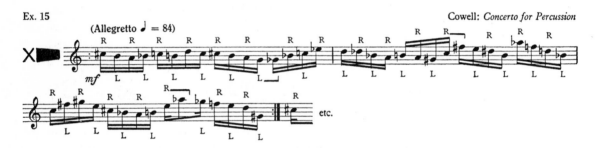

There are many ways of playing the above passage, but that shown indicates a fairly straightforward solution. The double beats have had to be included to avoid awkward cross-over hammerings when moving back and forth on to the rear row of keys (see later). However, as these double beats do not fit symmetrically into the musical design, the rhythmic flow will probably be disturbed. It is therefore best to avoid such situations if possible. The above passage is full of problems and the reader would do well to study it and try to find better solutions than the one shown. (In passing, it is worth drawing attention to the fact that this example is very typical of many pieces for xylophone. The highly chromatic successions of notes, weaving about in a small area, sound very effective indeed. But they are hard to play and require a great deal of study. One expert player confessed that he spent three years perfecting a very similar piece.)

Double beats are particularly difficult at speed when the same hand must play two notes widely separated. This is sometimes necessary in a passage as follows, where the seventh B—C♯ *must* be played by the left hand:

Ex. 16

Rather than write such an inconvenient passage, the composer would do well to reconsider the last three notes. By simply transposing one or two notes into different octaves, the double beat could be eliminated without much sacrifice to the musical sense.

When chords are used, as in the following example, very awkward double or triple beats become inevitable:

Ex. 17

Haubenstock-Ramati: *Symphonies de timbres*

When players have to deal with problems of this kind, they are apt to doubt whether the music's significance really justifies such difficulties. No wonder they often resort to octave transpositions so as to simplify their tasks.

Cross-over beats are very common, in fact unavoidable, in keyboard percussion playing. In any scale (both chromatic and diatonic) or arpeggio, the hammers must pass over each other, and a part of the performer's studies is specifically directed towards mastering the problems which arise. Yet difficulties crop up which are much better avoided at the composing stage. It is not easy to give precise rules, but in general it can be said that one hammer should be kept in front of the other within a passage. If the beaters have to change over their 'forward position' it is best to let a few notes intervene which will allow the player to swivel into the new position:

Ex. 18

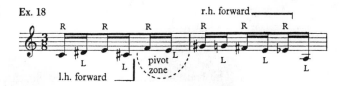

In this example the last two notes in the first bar act as a kind of 'pivot zone' in which the left beater is withdrawn, to cede its forward position to the right. For obvious reasons it is important to avoid situations in which the

beaters have to leap an excessive distance over each other, especially on the
larger instruments.

The worst cross-overs to be avoided are those where the beaters have no
chance to exchange their forward position, and risk becoming entangled:

If this passage is played using alternate beaters, there are several cross-
overs where the sticks 'get in each other's way' whichever hand begins. In
fact it is quite impossible to play this passage with alternate hands. The
reader is left to discover the difficult cross-overs for himself, so that he can be
better aware of the problems involved. Of course these difficulties could be
eliminated by introducing double beats (e.g. on the third and fourth notes of
each bar, if the left hand begins), and in general any good player can work out
hammerings which will get him through most difficulties. But it would be
better if composers and orchestrators were to write only what is suited to
keyed percussion, so that performers have no need to make the best of a bad
job.

The Tremolo
The tremolo or roll is very effective with keyed percussion, particularly on
the vibraphone and marimba because of their more sustained sounds. The
tremolo is performed by a succession of rapidly repeated beats and may be
executed on one note only, or on two, three, or four different notes. Tremolos
can produce a sustained melody of expressive character:

The tremolo is usually indicated by three inclined strokes through the
stems, as shown above. This is preferable to the abbreviation 'tr.' sometimes
used, which can be easily confused with the conventional trill between two
adjacent notes.

Sustained two-note chords can be rolled with good effect. These should be shown as in (a) below. The notation shown in (b) is sometimes used, but it is less clear and economical:

Ex. 21

Percussion players are, in any case, well aware that the three inclined strokes are used to indicate a freely-timed tremolo and not reiterated notes in exact tempo.

Tremolos on three or four notes are characteristic of the vibraphone and marimba, giving a full-bodied 'organ' tone with soft beaters. If two beaters are held in each hand, it is possible to alter the number of notes in each chord (see below) so that two-, three- and four-note tremolos can be freely mixed, provided the music is reasonably straightforward. In this case it is important to show which notes are to be played by each hand, by writing upward and downward stems (right and left hand respectively):

Ex. 22

Chords of three or more notes

If players are required to use three or four hammers, they must naturally be given a few bars' rest to take up the extra beaters. A span of up to an octave or more may be written for either hand, though it is best to use more comfortable intervals.

Even when a performer is using two beaters in each hand it is still possible to play passages in single notes. This is done by tilting the hand so that only one beater strikes the keys.

Not all note-combinations are easy. Those to avoid, if at all possible, are chords which bring the wrists into contact. For example, if C D♯ and F♯ A are played, both hands have to be turned outwards at a sharp angle and the wrists brought right together. Players often keep the span of the beaters constant, and reduce or augment the intervals played by turning the wrists, so it is particularly important in four-note writing to keep to note combinations in which the wrists can be kept sufficiently apart.

Rapid successions of chords are easy if the span of the beaters in each hand can be kept constant, especially in scale-like passages. But if the span of the beaters in each hand needs considerable modification, the player must be given time to do this. The same is true where big changes of wrist angle are necessary.

It is possible to use three hammers in either hand, for playing five- or six-note chords. The player must be given ample time to prepare the position of the beaters, and the notes played by each hand should be close together and preferably on the same row of keys. For instance, E F and G can be easily played by either hand, but D E♭ and G♭ is an altogether different story! Multi-note chords can be particularly effective in producing strong dynamic effects. For instance, note clusters formed by playing say G♭ A♭ and B♭ with the left hand, and A B and C with the right are most impressive in fortissimo.

Glissandos

These are a commonplace in keyboard percussion music, but nevertheless are of excellent effect. Glissandos can be played on either row of bars. Players prefer to execute a glissando on the natural keys with the left hand, while the right hand attacks the first and final notes sharply. On the rear row of keys glissandos sound 'broken', as of course there are only five notes to each octave. So when a glissando is indicated from one sharp or flat note to another, players prefer to strike the initial and final notes with the right hand and play the glissando on the *natural* keys with the left. However, if glissandos are definitely required on the rear row of keys, the right hand should be used for upward glissandos and the left hand reserved only for downward glissandos. Otherwise there is a danger that a beater will be caught in a gap between the keys and go flying through the air!

Glissandos on the rear row of keys come off more easily on the xylophone than on other instruments.

Sometimes glissandos are written out in full:

Ex. 23

Messiaen: *Oiseaux Exotiques*

but it is much more usual to indicate the first and last notes played, and connect them by a straight or wavy line with the indication 'gliss.':

Ex. 24

Kelemen: *Transfigurationen*

Other forms of glissando are sometimes indicated in a free manner, by a graphic design which gives only a general indication of the composer's requirements. Some of these are shown below:

Ex. 25

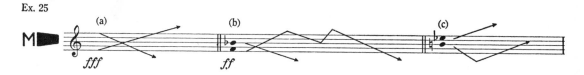

(a) shows a double glissando in opposite directions with both sticks. The starting and finishing points are not indicated. (b) and (c) indicate glissandos on both rows of keys beginning on the notes indicated and following the paths shown by the arrows.

Aleatory indications

Occasionally composers make some graphic design which gives performers an approximate idea of what to play over a certain time period. For instance, in the following example from Berio's *Circles*, the performer is given an outline design for an extremely rapid passage on wood chimes and marimba. The general contours are clearly indicated, but the precise notes are left to chance, except the final trill on F♯ and G:

Ex. 26

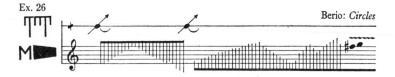

Berio: *Circles*

Such aleatory passages can be extremely effective, and have a great advantage in that the performer can play very rapid successions of notes without the encumbrance of reading precise notation.

Octave transpositions

In order to avoid the use of a large number of leger-lines, keyed percussion parts are often transposed an octave lower or higher and indicated '8va sopra' or '8va sotto', respectively. The transposition to an octave below is usually only necessary for the high register of the xylophone and the highest notes of the marimba, while transposition an octave higher is not needed except for the lowest notes of the marimba when the bass clef is not used. As it is customary to write glockenspiel parts two octaves lower than the actual sounds, no octave or double-octave transpositions need be indicated.

XYLOPHONE AND XYLOMARIMBA. MARIMBA. VIBRAPHONE

GLOCKENSPIEL, BELL LYRA AND KEYBOARD GLOCKENSPIEL

CELESTA. DULCITONE

Xylophone and Xylomarimba

The modern xylophone has a set of hardwood bars laid out in piano-keyboard fashion. The accidentals are usually raised to facilitate the playing of rapid passages, but occasionally they may be level with the natural keys. The bars are usually all the same width, being about 1¾ in. (4.4 cm.) wide and ⅞ in. (2.2 cm.) thick.

Not long ago, xylophones were made without resonators, so that the tone was characteristically dry and brittle. Today however they are usually fitted with tuned tubular metal resonators. These give a richer and more sustained tone, but are usually limited in size as compared with those of the marimba, for it is important not to lose the characteristic sharp, hard tone. The marimba has a mellow, booming tone, and it is in composers' interests to retain this difference.

Xylophones are made with a range of between two and a half and four octaves. Large 'virtuoso' models have a compass of four octaves ascending from middle C:

However, a three-and-a-half-octave model is quite suitable for most orchestral needs, and as this instrument is more likely to be found in orchestras than the cumbersome larger one, it is best to write within the following compass:

Xylophone parts are often written an octave below the real sounds, but it is becoming customary to write at the actual pitch. It would be best to add a note to this effect in the score, otherwise there can be a great deal of confusion.

The xylomarimba (or 'xylorimba') is a large xylophone sometimes specified in modern scores. There is some confusion as to the exact nature of this instrument. Some scores call for the 'xylorimba' (e.g. Stockhausen's *Gruppen*) where it would seem that only the large four-octave xylophone is required. The xylomarimba covers the full range of both marimba and xylophone. It is normally a five-octave instrument, though four-and-a-half-octave models are frequent. The range is as follows.

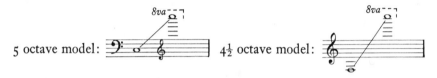

5 octave model: 4½ octave model:

It was popular with soloists of the music hall type because of its impressive appearance and because its wide range gave increased variety and contrast to their repertoire. But the instrument is not favoured by contemporary players because of its cumbersome size, nor is it part of the normal equipment of concert orchestras.

The bass xylophone made for Orff-Schulwerk would make a useful lower extension to the xylophone. It is not cumbersome, having a compass of only an octave and a sixth from C below middle C to the A above. The instrument is made in two parts, one with diatonic notes, the other with the chromatic bars. In addition, bars can be easily changed over. For example, if a piece is only in G major, F sharps can be substituted for the F naturals, and only the one row of diatonic bars need be set up. The instrument has an excellent tone, rather on the mellow side.

Keyboard xylophones have occasionally been scored for, but as I have found no trace of their commercial production today, it would seem best to ignore their existence. In any case, their tone was decidedly inferior to that of normal models, and only one tone colour was possible.

There is a wide variety of mallets available for use with the xylophone. Traditionally, the instrument was played with a pair of spoon-shaped wooden beaters, but these have now been replaced by a variety of round-headed beaters varying from hard wood, ebonite, and vulcanized rubber (for loud passages and a more brittle tone) to medium and soft rubber or felt (for quieter and more mellow effects). The player may be left to choose mallets suitable to the scale of dynamics. But beaters can be indicated if a specific kind of tone is required. Hard beaters reinforce the higher harmonics, so that passages often give the impression of sounding one or even two octaves higher than their true pitch. Contact sounds too are particularly strong with hard beaters.

Xylophone players are often specialists in their own instrument, and as this has acquired a rather exhibitionist reputation, they have developed a brilliant technique. They can execute scales and arpeggios with admirable virtuosity. Trills, tremolos, and rapid figurations seem to roll off the instrument with astonishing ease and clarity. But the somewhat inexpressive tonal character of the instrument has perhaps encouraged a type of virtuosity which is not always deeply musical. Perhaps too, composers have been at fault in writing brilliant banalities, which, though highly suited to the instrument, have only a superficial emotive significance.

Nevertheless, the xylophone's genius does lie in its brilliance, its vitality in tone and movement. Often enough, this is exploited in continuous running passages which combine chromatic and diatonic scales with arpeggios, as in Henry Cowell's Concerto for Percussion:

Ex. 27

Cowell: *Concerto for Percussion*

Messiaen, however, has exploited this brilliance in a less conventional way in his imitation of tropical birds in *Oiseaux Exotiques*:

Ex. 28

Messiaen: *Oiseaux Exotiques*

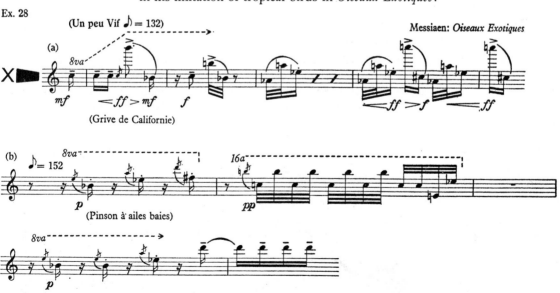

(c)

(Troglodyte de la Caroline)

Here the wide leaps, rapidly reiterated notes, grace notes, and dynamic contrasts are ideally suited to the instrument, while the rather hackneyed 'scale and arpeggio' style is avoided. Note the preference for the upper registers of the instrument, and the octave and double-octave transpositions. (These examples have been taken from the full score, which is written entirely at actual pitch. Messiaen's xylophone parts as used in the orchestra are written an octave lower than the real sounds. Note his use of '16ª' instead of '15ª'.)

The xylophone can be used for colouristic effects, as in Bartók's Music for Strings, Percussion, and Celesta, where it introduces the nostalgic, nocturnal atmosphere of the third movement with repeated notes, suggesting some night bird or creature of the insect world.

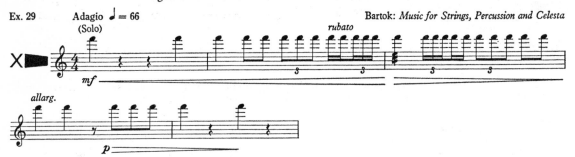

Ex. 29

Britten's 'Moonlight' interlude in the opera *Peter Grimes* makes excellent colouristic use of the xylophone. While most of the orchestra holds pulsating chords depicting the surge of the sea, the xylophone unites with the flute, piccolo, and harp in suggesting flashes of reflected light on the wavetops:

Ex. 30

But colouristic use of the xylophone is not always reserved for such tranquil scenes. The instrument can contribute a sure touch of the macabre, or give the music a twist towards the grotesque, as in Stravinsky's outlandishly orchestrated Saraband in *Agon*:

Apart from its melodic and colouristic potentialities, the xylophone is invaluable for its ability to add a hard percussive edge to dynamic effects played by the rest of the orchestra. These may have a melodic shape, as in Walton's *Belshazzar's Feast*:

Ex. 32   Walton: *Belshazzar's Feast*

or they may be isolated chords, or reiterated figurations:

Ex. 33   Chou Wen-Chung: *All in the Spring Wind*

Glissando effects are very brilliant on the xylophone, and can produce a considerable volume of sound. Various types of glissando have already been shown in Chapter 6, so there is little to add on this subject, except possibly to urge a little restraint in the use of this effect. It has already been used so much that there is a danger that it may become as hackneyed as the harp glissando.

Three- and four-hammer playing on keyboard percussion has also been discussed in Chapter 6, and most of these remarks are valid for writing for the xylophone, Three- and four-hammer playing is most effective on this instrument, either for percussive chords, sustained tremolos, or melodic passages filled out with harmony.

We must however take care not to ask the impossible in fast three- and four-hammer sections. The light-music repertoire of xylophone players features brilliant pieces for four-hammer playing, but it is noticeable that in rapid passages the beaters in each hand usually have a mean span of a third, which is extended to no more than a fourth, or reduced to a second wherever necessary. Awkward changes of wrist angle for playing accidentals are reduced to a minimum. With these factors taken into account, a four-hammer passage such as the following should not present great obstacles, and would come off brilliantly:

Ex. 34

The xylophone must be used carefully in ensemble work with other tuned percussion. Some composers (e.g. Messiaen) use it in combination with the marimba, vibraphone, and glockenspiel. But the xylophone is so much more powerful and penetrating than these other instruments that it dominates them completely. If it is used in such ensembles, soft beaters should be indicated and the dynamics 'marked down'.

Marimba

The modern marimba has found its way into Europe from America in a form which has obviously been influenced by the already-perfected xylophone. The keyboard layout is very similar, the compass is practically the same (though sounding an octave lower), the mechanism and mounting virtually identical.

The keyboard is made up of rosewood bars graduated in length according to pitch, with the accidentals raised above the level of the natural keys. The bars are usually graduated in width, being about $2\frac{1}{2}$ in. (6.5 cm.) wide at the low notes, reducing to 1¾ in. (4.5 cm.) wide in the upper register. The thickness of the bars can vary between ¾ and 15/16 of an inch (about 2 cm.).

Below each bar is fitted a vertical tubular metal resonator, tuned to the pitch of the bar. These resonators are much bigger than those fitted to xylophones, and their length and large diameter contribute to the rich depth of tone which is so characteristic of this instrument.

Marimbas have a fairly standard range of four octaves, ascending from tenor C:

This compass is occasionally exceeded: in America, some instruments descend to low A below tenor C, while on the Continent, occasional models reach up to F, a fourth higher than the compass shown above.

Such large instruments, however, are very unwieldy, and some three-octave models are becoming available. As these omit the upper octave, which is the least characteristic part of the marimba's compass (and therefore of less interest to the composer) there is a possibility that they may become more favoured.

A bass marimba is made in America by J. C. Deagan, Inc. The range is only one octave and a fourth, from C an octave below tenor C, to F above tenor C:

Bass marimbas have exceptionally large bars and resonating tubes. In order to avoid raising the keyboard, the resonators are bent upwards into 'U' shapes, like doubled-up organ pipes. These instruments are played with very large, heavy mallets, and as they are slow in response are not suited to quick-moving roles.

Marimba parts are written at their true pitch, the bass clef being necessary for the lowest portion of the keyboard. The upper notes can be transposed down an octave and indicated 'all'8va sopra', in order to avoid using too many leger-lines.

The characteristic tone of the marimba is mellow and soft, yet with a certain rich firmness. The lower portion of the instrument in particular has a deep 'boom', which builds up in tremolos to a beautifully sonorous, sustained tone. The upper register of the marimba has a less characteristic timbre, and lacks the firm, full tone of the lower portion of the instrument.

The marimba is usually played with soft mallets. Yarn-covered beaters with soft cores give the most characteristic tone, while medium-hard heads in yarn, felt, or rubber are used for a firmer tone and greater volume. Specially soft beaters are sold for playing in the low register, or timpani sticks can be quite effective.

Hard beaters should not be used on the marimba, as the bars may be damaged. In any case, they could only be called for in an attempt to force the volume, or to obtain a hard tone like the xylophone. In these circumstances, it would be best to abandon the marimba in favour of the xylophone.

The marimba has only entered into Western concert music comparatively recently, so the repertoire for the instrument is still fairly limited. It is suited to rapid passage work, though due to its great size (instruments can be seven feet long) it is naturally more limited in this respect than the xylophone. However, whereas the xylophone's rapidity is suited to brilliant effects, the marimba is ideal for liquid, rippling passages of a more subdued nature:

Ex. 35 Berio: *Circles*

The four-hammer tremolo is particularly effective, producing a smooth legato sound which is warm and full, and rightly merits the term 'organ tone'. Such marimba tremolos can be used to provide the entire harmonic core of the music, as a background to melody and other figurations:

Ex. 36

Soft tremolos can give a wonderful pulsation to sustained orchestral chords, without the sound of the marimba being evident:

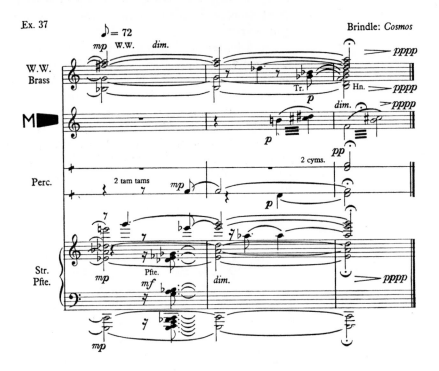

Ex. 37   Brindle: *Cosmos*

The soft percussive effect of staccato marimba chords is quite unique. In such a passage as the following, the deep throb of the marimba chords can be produced by no other instrument:

Ex. 38

Various aspects of writing for marimba (hammerings, multi-note chords, glissandos, and aleatory indications) have already been discussed in Chapter 6 on writing for keyboard percussion. Possibly the only additional comment to be made is on the glissando. If soft yarn beaters are used, the volume of the glissando will be relatively small, especially in the upper register. So if a fair volume of sound is required, the glissando should be marked 'forte' and the performer will use a somewhat harder set of beaters.

Vibraphone

The vibraphone was developed in America in the early 'twenties, most probably from the glockenspiel. There, it early found favour in the jazz field, but for some considerable time symphonic composers fought shy of what has been called its 'exaggerated sweetness'. Berg used it in his opera *Lulu* (1934–5), but the instrument only came into symphonic and chamber music after the Second World War. By now, however, the vibraphone (or vibraharp, as it is often called in the USA) is recognized as probably the most expressive and versatile percussion instrument, capable of solo melody, accompaniment, the creation of atmospheres, or simply the reinforcement of dynamics.

The standard vibraphone has a range of three octaves:

Both larger and smaller instruments have been made (four octaves beginning at C below middle C, or two and a half octaves from middle C). But as the three octave model is by far the commonest, there is not much point in writing for other instruments.

'Soprano' vibraphones are made, with a range one octave higher than normal, as an economical substitute for both vibraphone and glockenspiel.

If it is necessary to extend the range of the vibraphone a few notes lower, the bass metallophone made for Orff-Schulwerk can be used. Like the bass xylophone it has a compass of an octave and a sixth upwards from C below middle C. Similarly, it is made in two parts (natural bars and chromatic bars). The tone is full and mellow.

There has been some controversy as to the actual pitch of the vibraphone. Occasionally composers have believed vibraphone sounds to be an octave above the pitch generally recognized, and they have scored accordingly. Given the strong octave harmonics which characterize vibraphone sounds, there is perhaps some basis for this belief, and this matter will be mentioned again later.

Vibraphones have a keyboard made of two layers of aluminium alloy bars, with diatonic notes in the first row near the player and chromatic notes in the second row. Both rows of bars are always level with each other, to facilitate four-mallet playing. The bars are usually $\frac{1}{2}$ in. (1.27 cm.) thick and may all be the same width (about $1\frac{1}{2}$ in. (3.8 cm.)) or may be graduated from about $2\frac{1}{4}$ in. (5.7 cm.) wide in the low register to $1\frac{1}{2}$ in. (3.8 cm.) in the upper.

All the bars have tubular metal resonators fitted below them, tuned to the same pitch as the bars. The keyboard and resonators are usually chromium-plated or gold anodized.

Normally the bars lie on felt dampers, so that when they are struck, the sounds are staccato and rather 'choked' and lifeless. The bars are lifted off the dampers by a 'damper pedal' (really a 'sustaining pedal') fitted below the instrument, and long enough to be operated by either foot. The player uses the damper pedal whenever notes are struck, but takes care to damp off notes which, by ringing on, would only confuse the melody or harmony. Damping will be further discussed later.

The tops of the resonators are fitted with discs which can be made to revolve by means of an electric or clockwork motor, thus alternately opening and closing the tubes. This produces the characteristic 'vibrato' of the vibraphone, a vibrato which really comprises two factors—fluctuations in pitch and variations in volume.

The electric motor actuating the discs is usually of variable speed, so that different rates of vibrato are possible. This has its abuses. Some players prefer a very slow vibrato, which can cause rather unpleasant pitch fluctuations. Others like a fast vibrato which makes the sound shudder. However, these effects can be useful and desirable in the right place, and it is not unusual for composers to indicate 'slow vib.', 'medium vib.', or 'fast vib.' in their scores, where such effects are appropriate.

The vibraphone can be effectively used without vibrato. This gives a cool, level sound of virgin quality which is quite in contrast with the warmth of vibrato tone. To play the instrument without vibrato the player has to switch off the motor and turn the discs so that the resonating tube ends are open (otherwise the sound is too dead). There should therefore be a short rest in the player's part to allow him to do this. Where vibrato or non-vibrato are required, this is usually indicated in the part by the words 'motor on' or 'motor off'.

An excellent effect can be produced by playing a note or chord with the motor off, and then setting it in motion at gradually increasing speed. The note or notes are first level and cool; then, as the sound dies, it begins to tremble with the increasing vibrato.

The vibraphone is usually played with soft beaters, as these produce the mellow tone most characteristic of the instrument. In this case the beaters will probably have soft-core wool-wound heads. However, the instrument can produce a brilliant, ringing tone with harder hammers, which may have hard felt or rubber heads.

For general use, beaters with yarn- or cord-wound heads are advisable. Their cores can have different degrees of hardness, thus providing different tonal effects, attack characteristics, and degrees of volume. Vibraphone players prefer such beaters to all others, for they give the best tone and eliminate contact sounds. Wound beaters with soft cores can be indicated thus: ♀ , and those with hard cores: ♀ .

Sticks with heads made of hard plastic produce a penetrating metallic sound, which can cut through an orchestral tutti. Sometimes metal beaters are indicated, but when used forcibly these damage the soft alloy bars, and in any case only produce the same sound as hard plastic beaters. However, metal glockenspiel beaters can be used in quiet passages, if a distinctly metallic effect is required.

More than on almost any other instrument, different kinds of mallets produce not only different volumes of sound on the vibraphone, but different *qualities* of sound. Hard beaters indeed reinforce the upper partials so much that—as mentioned above—some composers have thought the instrument sounds an octave higher than the pitch usually recognized.

Some composers leave the player to choose whatever mallets are most suitable to the dynamics indicated or the general musical situation. Others indicate each kind of mallet required, in considerable detail. But perhaps the best method is to give the player a general indication of the kind of stick to use (e.g. 'soft sticks', 'hard sticks', etc.) and leave him to make his own choice as to the exact kind to use. This is important, as in some passages players use a slightly harder mallet in the right hand in order to make higher notes equal in volume to lower notes.

The vibraphone is particularly suited to slow-moving, expressive melody as at (a) below. The melody can be made even more sustained in character by the use of tremolo as at (b):

In addition, by using two, three, or four beaters, a melody may be harmonized with or without the tremolo, as at (a) and (b) below:

Ex. 40 (a)
Adagio

(b)

In the above example, a harder hammer is indicated for the right hand, so that the melody will stand out.

In a flowing melody, grace notes and embellishments can be freely used. Not only do they suit the nature of the instrument very well, they give a fuller effect and impulse to the melodic line:

Ex. 41
Andante

Grace notes can be used to form chords:

Ex. 42
Lento

The fourth chord in the above example could of course be written as an arpeggio. Naturally, the sustaining pedal would have to be used for each of these chords, but its use is so obvious that it need not be specially indicated.

The contrast of single notes, arabesques, and tremolos is most effective:

Ex. 43
Moderato

etc.

From the end of the third bar on, the pianissimo tremolo is maintained as a quiet background to the melody in isolated notes, played much louder. In this way the vibraphone can provide its own 'background' accompaniment, with a 'foreground' melody which emerges on an altogether different dynamic plane.

In the last example it will be seen that the first two tremolos are begun with grace notes. This gives a better effect, particularly in the case of the second tremolo, where the cascade of notes gives a fine attack, sweeping down to the *sforzando* F♯. Without these embellishments, the tremolos would be rather naked and banal.

Though the vibraphone is better suited to slow-moving music than the xylophone and marimba, there is no reason why it should not be used in rapid, energetic passages. Especially if hard beaters are used, and provided the damper pedal is not used much, the effect will be crisp and shining:

Ex. 44

Whether to include indications for the use of the damper pedal is a little problematical. Sometimes it is absolutely necessary to indicate how the pedal should be used but normally players can be left to use their own judgement. Perhaps the best precedent to follow is that adopted for the piano. There only essential or unusual pedalling indications are given. For the rest, the player uses his own good sense, interpreting the information on the printed page in a conventional musical fashion.

The whole matter hinges on the need to keep parts as graphically simple as possible. Perhaps the best solution is to use slurs between those notes which can be played in the same 'pedalling', all other notes then being separated, or at the most, 'half-pedalled'. To illustrate this method, we will take an excerpt from Milko Kelemen's *Equilibres*:

Ex. 45

Kelemen: *Équilibres*

Here, in an effort to show that certain note groups are sustained with the pedal, Kelemen has resorted to a complex form of notation—one has to look at the music more than once to see what is intended. Unfortunately, though this notation reveals eventually that full pedallings are needed on the first and last beats of the first bar and the third beat of the second bar, there is no information as to whether the remaining notes are separated or whether they may be slurred into groups. Obviously, if some pedalling is not used, the effect is bound to be dry and unmusical.

If however, slurs are used to show which groups of notes are to be pedalled together, the notation is considerably simplified. The player is left in no doubt as to which notes can be merged together and which must be separated:

Ex. 46

It will be noticed that, in the first note-group, to be faithful to Kelemen's original the C has had to be separated off from the other sounds. This can only be done by 'finger damping'.

Finger damping overcomes one of the big limitations of the vibraphone. It permits the stopping of notes, or the resolution or substitution of a note or notes within a chord while it is being held, without releasing the sustaining pedal or re-striking the chord. After striking a chord, a note may be substituted for another by simultaneously striking a new note and damping the old note with a finger:

Ex. 47

This gives a natural flow and clear smoothness to the music which is otherwise impossible.

Boulez uses this technique to excellent effect in his *Une Dentelle s'Abolit*:

Ex. 48

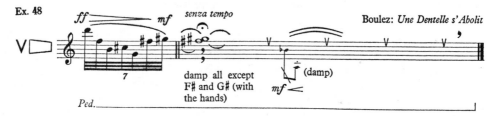

Here, all but two notes of the first arabesque are damped 'with the hands'. While these two notes are then sustained, two further notes are played staccato, being immediately damped with the fingers. The sustaining pedal is shown depressed throughout. This is the kind of occasion when it is absolutely necessary to indicate exact pedallings.

Finger damping is therefore an important technical means by which an intricate 'counterpoint of sounds' can be produced, giving effects which are more subtle and musically elaborated than those usually written for this instrument.

Multiple-note chords are particularly effective on the vibraphone, the resulting sound being rich and full, especially when vibrato is used. Information on writing chords of three or more notes has already been given in Chapter 6 and only one additional point needs to be made. Chords for the vibraphone are so frequently written with the notes bunched together in 'close order', and so rarely with a wide spread, that many composers must be convinced that only close chords are possible, or that only this type of chord sounds well.

Certainly, close chords have a homogeneous sound, though this is not always of vital importance. But in widely spread chords the component sounds are more distinct, and the dissonances (if any) are smoothed out. The following are a few of the spread chords to be found in Boulez's *Dentelle*:

Ex. 49

It will be seen that, in most of these chords, dissonances (especially semitones) are widely separated, so that they are less harsh, and that in the last three chords Boulez has taken advantage of the fact that each hand can be widely separated to produce four-note chords with two notes low down and two high up. In such well-spread chords, it is best to indicate harder hammers in the right hand, so that a good balance is obtained.

Glissandos are very effective on the vibraphone. As with the xylophone, brilliant splashes of sound can be produced by the various methods discussed in Chapter 6. But in addition, the vibraphone can give very subtle atmospheres with soft glissandos, producing effects which are quite unique to this instrument.

In all the normal glissando effects mentioned in Chapter 6, the beaters must be stroked *rapidly* over the keys to produce adequate volume, so that inevitably the actual glissando lasts for only a brief moment of time. The vibraphone however, can sustain all the notes struck when the foot-pedal is depressed.

But the vibraphone can also be made to produce two types of *slow* glissando, by which the actual glissando effect can be considerably prolonged. One method is to sweep the beaters repeatedly over a limited area of the natural keys, usually beginning in the low register, and then moving over the keyboard slowly into the upper register. The sustaining pedal is used, so that all the sounds merge, and the precise successions of notes are not over-evident. This effect is most successful at low volume, and the use of vibrato will help to fuse the sounds into a mysterious, trembling atmosphere. It would be indicated by either of the following methods:

Ex. 50

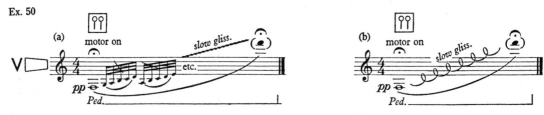

Naturally, this form of glissando can be used either ascending or descending. In addition, both beaters can begin in the centre of the instrument and move outwards, or begin at the extremities of the keyboard and move towards the centre.

The other slow glissando (the 'tremolo glissando') is performed by moving over the keyboard with the beaters playing tremolos on different notes. If two beaters are used in each hand, a fuller effect can be obtained. Naturally the beaters can move from left to right, right to left, from the centre outwards, from the extremities of the keyboard to the centre, and so on. It is advisable to use this effect too at low volumes (with the sustaining pedal, vibrato, and soft beaters) so that the actual note-successions are rather hidden. As the exact notes played are best left to the player's own invention, the tremolo glissando can be indicated by a graphic design showing the composer's approximate requirements, for example:

Ex. 51

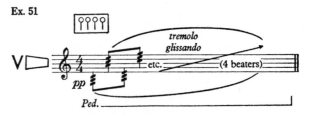

Occasionally composers indicate glissandos to be played on the resonating tubes. The sound produced is thin and tinny, with no real musical quality. The best effect is produced with the handle of a stick, or bamboo cane.

Glockenspiel or *Orchestral Bells*

The glockenspiel has two rows of steel bars arranged in the manner of a piano keyboard. It is usually contained in a portable case which can be set up on a table, the lid being removed to expose the keyboard. The rear row of bars is usually raised above the front layer. The steel bars are rectangular, between 1 in. and 1¼ in. (about 3 cm.) wide and ¼ in. to ⅜ in. (about 0.8 cm.) in thickness.

The glockenspiel has been made with a compass varying between two and three octaves, but today instruments have a fairly standard range of two and a half octaves, written G to C as follows, but sounding two octaves higher:

Unlike the vibraphone, the glockenspiel is not normally fitted with tubular resonators, and there is no damping mechanism. The bars are mounted in a manner which allows the notes to ring free and clear, so that in rapid passages the sounds overlap each other, blurring the phrase outlines, but producing that shining aura which is such a valuable characteristic of this instrument.

Occasionally, in order to eliminate the confusing ring of the glockenspiel's sounds, the instrument is 'muted' or muffled by laying a light cloth over part of the bars.

The glockenspiel is played with a variety of mallets or beaters. For quiet effects, beaters with soft rubber knobs are used. For normal volumes, medium to hard rubber ends are required, while a variety of beaters are available for forte passages—ebonite, wood, horn, plastic, etc. Metal beaters, with brass balls mounted on plexiglass sticks, are available where a strong, clear sound is called for in forte passages. However, these must be used only on glockenspiels with steel bars, not on instruments with alloy bars. Normally, the choice of suitable beaters is left to the player's discretion. Glockenspiel parts seldom give any indication of the composer's requirements except in very special cases.

Because of the glockenspiels's sparkling crystal tones, the instrument has been almost exclusively used to contribute to brilliant sonorities or luminous atmospheres. By reason of the brief duration, limited volume and relative indefiniteness of its sounds, the glockenspiel is rarely used to contribute in a decisive way to harmonic structures. Even in melody, it is very often doubled by another instrument so as to give greater continuity and body to the sound. For instance, even in Henry Cowell's Concerto for Percussion and Orchestra (where one might expect to see the glockenspiel play a free melodic role to some extent) the instrument is always doubled to give the melody more clarity:

Ex. 52   Cowell: *Concerto for Percussion*

The one major exception is shown in Ex. 72 where the addition of a wood-wind or string instrument would have spoiled the deliberately hard, shining sound of the passage.

The doubling of upper woodwind parts by the glockenspiel to give sparkle and brilliance is fairly commonplace. But particularly in rapid passages, where continuous glockenspiel sounds would tend to become confused, the instrument often outlines only the salient points of the melody, this being quite enough to give the desired brilliance:

Ex. 53   Ross Lee Finney: *Symphony No. 2*

However, the glockenspiel is ideally suited to solo passages where the general effect is deliberately fugitive, ephemeral, or evanescent:

Ex. 54

Brindle: *Homage to H. G. Wells*

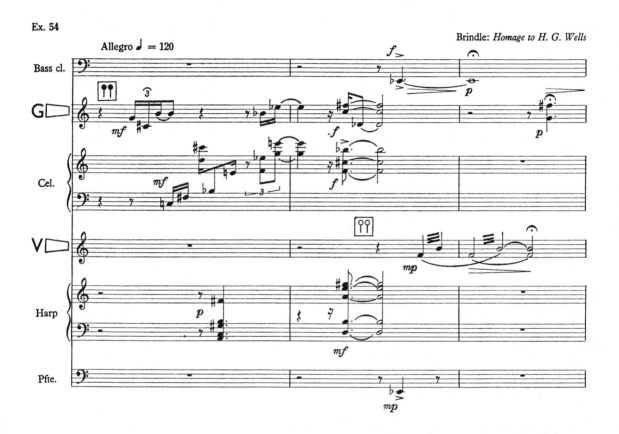

or where the composer deliberately wishes to create a dense medley of sounds. Many such passages occur in Messiaen's *Oiseaux Exotiques*, where each instrument imitates a particular bird-song, when they all join together in a stupendous counterpoint of brilliant chattering melodies. However in this and other works, Messiaen specifies a keyboard glockenspiel, for which see p. 58.

The instrument is invaluable for introducing tiny touches of light in accompaniments, either by short figures and arabesques, or by isolated sounds, as in the following example from Schoenberg's Variations, Op. 31.

Ex. 55   Langsam ♪= 120   Schoenberg: *Variations for Orchestra*

A shining background colour can be introduced against a dark orchestral foreground by quiet glockenspiel figurations. As Alan Hovhaness shows in his Concerto No. 8 for Orchestra, in such situations the instrument can be used at a different tempo from the rest of the orchestra, introducing notes which do not always belong to the orchestral harmony (as at 'a' below). At 'b' is shown a passage where almost all glockenspiel notes are foreign to the harmony:

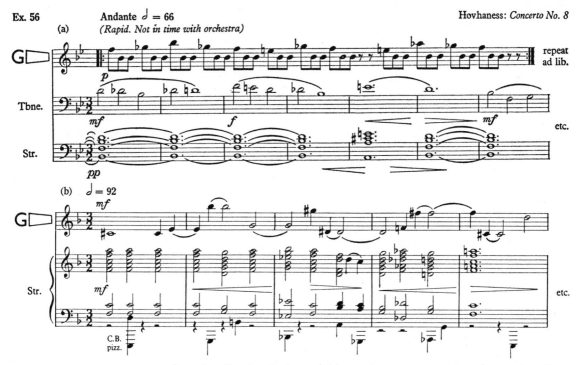

Ex. 56   Andante ♩ = 66   Hovhaness: *Concerto No. 8*

Occasionally the glockenspiel is used as an upper extension to the vibraphone. In the following example from Jean Barraqué's *Chant après Chant*, one player plays on both instruments:

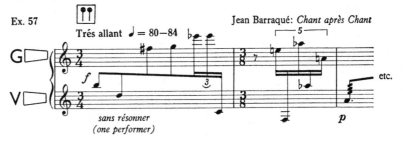

Ex. 57   Jean Barraqué: *Chant après Chant*

As with other keyboard percussion instruments, the glissando and tremolo can be used, particularly in forte passages. Three- and four-note chords are also possible though not frequently used.

The *bell lyra* or *lyra-glockenspiel* is a form of glockenspiel adapted for use in marching bands. The keyboard is held vertically (ladder-wise) in a lyre-shaped aluminium frame fixed to a staff carried by a special support in the player's belt. The instrument can be fixed vertically to a stand when not on the march, or played flat in a case like the normal glockenspiel.

Bell lyras have a more limited range than the glockenspiel, usually two octaves, but sounding two octaves higher:

Bell lyra   (sounds two octaves higher)

The instrument is usually played with hard plastic mallets, has great penetrating power, and can be heard above the forte of a large band.

The *keyboard glockenspiel* (the French 'jeu de timbres'), is rarely written for nowadays, perhaps because it is by no means a common instrument, perhaps because its tone and volume do not equal that of the conventional glockenspiel. Being enclosed in a box, the tone of the instrument is muffled. In addition, the keyboard mechanism permits the production of only one scale of volume; no nuances are possible, and usually the noisy mechanism gives a toylike effect. But though this instrument has been superseded by the celesta for soft effects and by the glockenspiel for brilliance, its keyboard allows the performance of chords, polyphonic passages, and very rapid figurations which are beyond the possibilities of the conventional instrument, such as the following:

Ex. 58   Messiaen: *Chronochromie*

Keyboard
Glock.

In such works as *Chronochromie* Messiaen always writes very swift single-note patternings. Chords and polyphony are excluded. The same is true of Stockhausen's use of this instrument in *Gruppen* except for very occasional chord passages as follows:

Ex. 59

Stockhausen: *Gruppen*

Keyboard
Glock.

In both the above works the keyboard glockenspiel is written for with a wide range of dynamics which cannot be reproduced. In addition there seems to be some miscalculation as to the volume scale of the instrument. At some points Messiaen writes *mf* for the keyboard glockenspiel against xylophone *ff*. Here and in many other passages the instrument is quite inaudible. Certainly the use of this instrument in Mozart's *The Magic Flute* seems better calculated.

The keyboard glockenspiel usually has a range of a little over three octaves, written as follows, but sounding two octaves higher:

Keyboard
Glockenspiel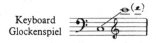

Celesta

This instrument is often not regarded as a percussion instrument. However, there is no doubt that it belongs to the family of tuned idiophones, and as in some modern scores the celesta is included amongst the percussionist's instruments (e.g. in Berio's *Circles*), there are reasonable grounds for including the celesta in the percussion group. In any case, though in orchestras the celesta is usually played by a pianist, it is important here to compare the possibilities of the celesta with similar idiophones such as the glockenspiel and dulcitone.

Invented about 1880 by the Parisian Mustel, the celesta is a form of glockenspiel fitted with a piano-type keyboard. Tuned steel bars of glockenspiel type are struck by hammers through the keyboard mechanism, and as each bar is fitted on a tuned wooden resonating box, the sound has a round but ethereal sweetness, which is quite different from the glockenspiel's brilliant, hard sparkle.

The gentle, soft tones of the celesta are of short duration, and the keyboard mechanism does not permit any useful graduations of volume. However, a sustaining foot-pedal is fitted on all instruments. Though this is often called the 'damper' pedal, staccato notes are impossible.

The range of the instrument is four octaves ascending from middle C, but the music is usually written an octave lower than the real sounds, using two staves:

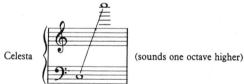

Celesta   (sounds one octave higher)

It is important to appreciate the small amount of sound emitted by the celesta. This can only be done by actually playing the instrument, when one's first impressions are that the keyboard is almost dead and not responding sufficiently to the touch. It is also important to insist that virtually no distinct graduations of volume are possible. Those composers who fill their celesta parts with pianissimos and fortissimos have obviously never had their hands on the instrument!

The celesta (unlike the glockenspiel) is easily covered by the rest of the orchestra, and should only be used in quiet passages, particularly if it has a solo role. Solo melody is very rarely given to the celesta in orchestral compositions. The sound is so evanescent that it is not suitable for slow-moving cantilenas, while in rapid-moving melodies the tendency for the sounds to run on and overlap each other causes a confused effect.

But composers have perhaps gone too far in avoiding celesta melodies. Where these are delicate and tenuous, with a gentle movement, the celesta can be used with confidence, providing the accompaniment is well subdued. In the following example from the opening of the author's Variations on a Theme of Dallapiccola, the theme is passed between the flute and celesta in a play of soft colours:

Ex. 60

Brindle: *Variations on a theme of Dallapiccola*

The above was not written without misgivings that the celesta sounds might prove to be too slight for the first announcement of thematic material. But such fears proved to be without foundation.

However, it is certain that the celesta is more suited (by the very nature of its sounds) to producing fugitive, decorative embroideries rather than making decisive statements. The slender tracery of its arabesques, in such passages as the following can hardly be produced by any other instrument:

Ex. 61   Brindle: *Variations on a theme of Dallapiccola*

The celesta is invaluable for delicate touches of chordal harmony, particularly in *pointilliste*-type orchestrations:

Ex. 62   Webern: *Six Pieces for Orchestra Op. 6*

A special quality of the celesta is its ability to create a backcloth of shining luminosity, without being heard with too much definition. No other instrument can produce such delicate haloes of sound as background colour, with running figurations such as the following:

Ex. 63   Bartók: *Music for Strings, Percussion and Celesta*

It is often used to give a delicate impact to pianissimo woodwind or string chords, imparting a luminous quality to the harmony which would otherwise be absent:

Ex. 64

Schoenberg: *Variations for Orchestra*

Doubling of woodwind or string melodies and harmonies is a frequent duty for the celesta. Often such doubling is turned into running passages, filling out the harmony with arpeggios and arabesques. In such situations the function of the instrument is primarily a colouristic one, giving warmth and lusciousness to the music, or imparting an air of grace and fantasy.

It is becoming increasingly used in chamber music. Here, its small scale of volume is no longer a defect, so the instrument can play a much more varied and prominent role than in symphonic music.

For reference to an instrument called the 'celestette' see under 'sistrum' (final paragraph).

Dulcitone (TYPOPHONE)

This keyboard instrument has a pianoforte action similar to the celesta, but the sound is produced by the hammers striking steel tuning forks fitted to a resonating board. Dampers are fitted to each fork, actuated by a foot pedal.

The dulcitone, as its name suggests, is soft and sweet, with a bell-like sound not unlike the celesta. However, it has a more sustained tone than the latter instrument, the lower registers having a prolonged hum which gives the impression of an attractive depth of timbre. But the tone cannot be forced. Like the celesta, large gradations of volume are not possible, and the instrument must only be used in soft passages.

The dulcitone can be used in the same musical situations as the celesta, giving grace and luminosity to the orchestral sound. However, it is rarely used in the orchestra due to its scarcity, and never seems to have entered into the realm of chamber music. This is unfortunate, for the dulcitone is an ideal chamber instrument and could very well play an important role in chamber ensembles.

The instrument does not seem to be made in any standard size, but the four octaves ascending from tenor C are usually available, and there is little call to go outside these limits:

Dulcitone

The instrument is sometimes called the 'typophone', following D'Indy's use of this term in the score of his *Chant de la Cloche* for orchestra.

TUBULAR BELLS. GONGS. CROTALES. MUSICAL SAW

FLEXATONE. GLASSES. STEEL DRUMS. SANZA

Tubular Bells

There have been numerous attempts to introduce various types of bells into the orchestra. Some have resembled church bells, other have consisted of metal plates or inverted saucer-shaped discs. But because of their scarcity and variety, it is impossible to make any remarks about them of general application.

The only bells to be considered here are the tubular bells or 'chimes'. Because of their light tone-quality they are not satisfactory substitutes for (or imitations of) large bells. Nevertheless their sound has become a valuable addition to the orchestral colour-spectrum, and in any case they can play a much more agile role than their larger cousins.

Tubular bells are made of brass tubes about 1½ in. (4 cm.) in diameter, usually chromium plated, and hung in a frame by their upper ends with cords. They are made in complete sets, suspended in keyboard fashion, with diatonic notes in front and chromatic ones in the rear. A damper mechanism is attached, operated by the foot, so that tubes may be damped whenever necessary.

They are usually eighteen in number, and range from middle C to F one octave and a fourth above. Some American models have twenty tubes, including high F♯ and G, but as these cannot be counted on with certainty, it is best to write for the smaller model:

Tubular bells

The sounds should be written at pitch. Some composers write the notes an octave lower in the belief that this is the real pitch of tubular bells. They may indeed have these low fundamental tones, but these are so weak, compared with the actual sounds we perceive in an orchestral setting, that this usage should be abandoned. Though composers have not infrequently written for bells above and below the range given above (e.g. Messiaen requires a two-octave instrument from F♯ below middle C), and extra tubes can sometimes be hired to accommodate these needs, more often performers transpose these extreme notes an octave up or down, so that they lie within the range of their instrument.

The bells are played by striking them at the top rim with a special rawhide mallet. It should be noted that when the bells are struck, they oscillate back and forth in the cord harness. The player thus has to watch the position of the tubes with care in order to strike them accurately. This means that he has to memorize the music in order to keep one eye on the conductor and the other on the tubes. Accordingly, it is only reasonable to write music which can be readily committed to memory. In any case, though tubular bells can be played fairly rapidly, they are most effective in a simple role and when used with economy.

Though the rawhide mallet brings out the bells' fullest tone, other beaters may be used. A metal beater or triangle stick can produce a hard metallic sound (cf. Holst's *The Planets* p. 119), while a soft felt stick will produce a mellow hum. In general, a hard beater will as usual accentuate the higher harmonics and a soft beater the fundamental tone.

If bells are struck at the middle of their length, there is less percussive attack than when they are struck at the normal beating spot at the upper rim. Though the general tone is the same, the sounds have a more gentle, humming character.

Some composers indicate the muting of bells with a cloth, while if the tubes are struck through a soft cloth with the mallet (without the cloth remaining in contact with the tubes), a mellow rounded tone can be produced with the upper partials subdued.

The use of bells in a realistic way (e.g. Britten's *Peter Grimes*, Puccini's *Tosca* and many other operas) is a commonplace, just as is their use to create a general religious atmosphere or an air of solemnity. But this noble instrument can be dissociated completely from the cloisters. In Stravinsky's *Les Noces* it fits in perfectly with the raw, uncouth atmosphere of pagan festivity, while in Hindemith's *Symphonic Metamorphoses*, it joins with the timpani in an episode of simple exuberance. One can go even further and insert it in the realm of abstract music with no fear that it will evoke religiosity (cf. Boulez's *Improvisations sur Mallarmé* and Varèse's *Ionisation*). It simply belongs to the family of metallic percussion of definite pitch.

The following example includes the most common chime effects:

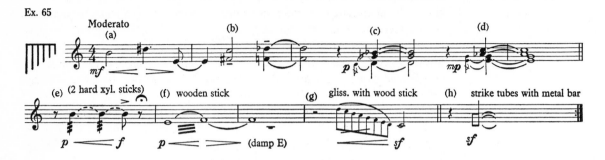

Ex. 65

(a) shows single notes and (b) two-note chords. In (c) and (d) three- and four-note chords are obtained by playing acciaccaturas on one or two notes, as the case may be.

In (e) a tremolo is played on one tube with two hard xylophone sticks. Tremolos can also be played with soft vibraphone beaters, or with two metal sticks (cf. the 'Sanctus' in Britten's *War Requiem*).

In (f) a wooden stick is inserted between two tubes so that a tremolo between two notes is obtained. At the end of the first bar the E is damped with the finger and the F allowed to ring on into the next bar without being struck separately.

Glissandos over the tubes can be very effective. In (g) an octave of diatonic notes are stroked downwards with a wooden stick in crescendo, while the low C is struck with a normal mallet. Alternatively, tubes can be stroked with a wire brush to give a soft metallic swish, or with a soft felt vibraphone beater for a mellow sound. A glissando over the tubes with a triangle beater gives a harsh clash of great effect. It must be noted that such glissandos are over the natural notes.

The last example (h) is not common, but very effective. Several tubes are struck horizontally with a metal bar or ruler, to give a very penetrating metallic clash.

Finally, the tubes can be played with the fingers for very quiet, subtle effects, and in this way a fair variety of timbre can be produced at a low volume scale which is ideal for chamber music.

Gongs

Gongs play an essential part in music of the Orient, where sets of tuned gongs (gong 'chimes' or 'plays') have been in common use for centuries. The art of gong making has now passed into Europe and America, but fine oriental instruments are possessed by some major symphony orchestras.

The gong is often confused with the tamtam, in fact it is certain that many composers have written 'gong' and 'tamtam' in their scores without appreciating their real differences (see 'tamtam' for further discussion regarding the nomenclature of these instruments).

Gongs are made from bronze alloy discs of heavier gauge than tamtams, so that for a given size the sound is much deeper and melodious, without the shrill overtones of the tamtam. Whereas the tamtam is flat or slightly saucer-shaped, and with a shallow rim, the gong usually has a surface area of more complex form, and a deep rim, sometimes of considerable depth. But the main feature of the gong is the fact that the centre is usually beaten out into a prominent protuberance or dome, by means of which the instrument is tuned. The more usual forms are as follows:

Fig. 4.

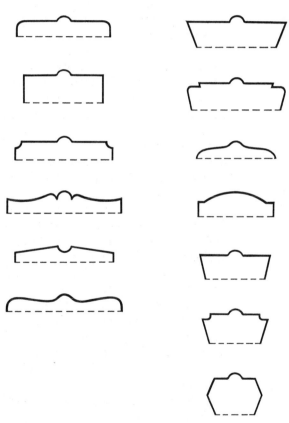

Gongs are normally tuned, but whereas some emit beautifully harmonious sounds, others are made to be rich in overtones of a more discordant nature, calculated to produce harsher tones, especially when struck forcibly, which may enter into the region of 'indeterminate sounds'. This latter type is fairly flat and has usually little or no protuberance, hence its confusion with the tamtam, and its inclusion in the category of instruments of indeterminate pitch. The gongs with a rounded dome are usually tuned to give a sonorous deep fundamental tone with harmonics of a concordant nature. Gongs with deep rims (particularly those in the right-hand column above), are often referred to as 'Chinese gongs' even though these forms are more typical of Java and Siam. Sets of tuned gongs of this type are used for the gong chimes which have such a thrilling effect in Puccini's *Turandot* and Mascagni's *Iris*. Some percussion ensembles have made up sets of tuned gongs for specially commissioned compositions, but there is no standard compass established so far. On the Continent such gong-plays are called 'Thailand gongs'.

Normally composers fight shy of using tuned gongs, as they could obviously play havoc with the orchestral harmonies. But there is no more majestic sound than a large tuned gong, and in music of an atonal nature there is so little risk of the harmonic equilibrium being disturbed that we need not hesitate to use such fine instruments. For instance, some of Messiaen's scores feature gongs very prominently and over long periods in a generally atonal context (e.g. *Et Expecto Resurrectionem Mortuorum* and *Chronochromie*), but he does not specify any tunings, merely instruments which sound in different registers.

Gongs are made in various sizes, the smallest suitable for normal orchestral use being about 20 in. (50 cm.) in diameter. Medium-sized instruments vary from 24 in. (61 cm.) to 28 in. (71 cm.) diameter and larger models from 30 to 38 in. (76 to 97 cm.).[1] They are usually hung from a circular steel support and struck with a special weighted wooden mallet covered with lamb's wool.

Sometimes composers indicate that the gong, after being struck, should be damped 'from the centre' so that the deeper tones are eliminated first, leaving the higher sounds ringing on until they too are damped. Sometimes they indicate that the gong should be struck with a timpani stick, thus producing a lighter tone, while occasionally a side drum stick is used (e.g. Stravinsky's *Petrushka*) to give a bright ringing sound, especially if struck on or near the rim. The gong may also be struck with a metal triangle beater (cf. Walton's *Belshazzar's Feast*) to give a hard, metallic clash.

A particularly harsh ringing sound can be produced by running a triangle beater round the rim of the gong with rapid sweeps, or across the surface on very large instruments.

[1] M.M. Paiste & Sohn make gongs from 7 in. diameter to 38 in. (18 to 97 cm.), and produce complete sets of gong chimes (thirteen instruments) for each of the four octaves beginning on low C, two octaves below middle C, and extending up to two octaves above middle C—a quite astonishing range. These gongs are made at Rendsburg, Germany but are sold through the firm's cymbal factory at Nottwil, Lucerne, in Switzerland.

The finest gong tone is produced with a heavy blow near the centre, using a large soft mallet. The sound is not produced instantaneously, but builds up to its maximum after a brief moment. If it is necessary for the maximum sound to coincide exactly with that of other instruments it is therefore advisable to indicate the stroke of the gong a fraction previously (say a semi-quaver in medium tempo).

The full power of the gong can best be built up by a tremolo or repeated strokes—in fact very large instruments definitely need a succession of strokes to give their full volume. This will be heard as a gradual crescendo, rather than as a succession of repeated notes. In the following example from Carlos Chavez's Toccata for Percussion Instruments, a very effective crescendo is built up by a cymbal roll and semiquaver beats on a small gong, ending with a fortissimo stroke on a large gong:

Ex. 66

Chávez: *Toccata for Percussion*

The gong has a very versatile nature. The right instrument can emit a majestic boom which creates an atmosphere of immense grandeur; played with hard or metal sticks on the rim it can produce a violent clash of sparkling sounds. But some of the most subtle effects can be created in quiet passages by soft strokes, which though hardly heard, build up a mysterious throbbing vibration in the orchestral texture.

An impressive passage in which the player elicits a great variety of tones from a single gong occurs at one of the most intense moments of Stockhausen's *Kontakte* for electronic sounds, percussion, and piano:

Ex. 67   Stockhausen: *Kontakte*

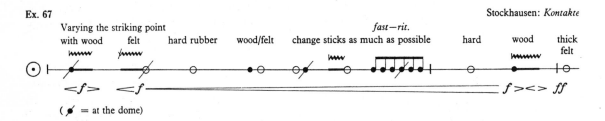

As will be seen, the player is instructed to strike the instrument at various points as well as on the dome, with various beaters. The duration of the passage is 40.2 seconds, and in the following section the gong is joined by the tamtam (played by the pianist) who has similar instructions. The effect is cataclysmic.

Gongs continue to sound for some time after being struck, so the termination of the sound should be accurately notated. If the sound is not to be damped, it is sufficient to indicate a tie on the note struck, with no note following, or use the letters 'L.V.' (lasciar vibrare).

If the performer has to use the heavy mallet, it is best to give him time to grasp this and get himself into a good playing position. In other words, he should not be expected to play the side drum one moment and the gong the next. His only solution would be to hit the gong with a stick which would be much too light and hard to produce the proper tone.

Mention must be made of the 'water gong' included in some modern scores. This is an effect obtained by immersing a gong in water when it is struck. As the instrument is lowered into the water there is a pronounced glissando downwards. When a gong is half submerged, its sound is an octave lower than normal. Completely immersed, it sounds two octaves lower. However, the more the gong is submerged, the weaker is the fundamental tone compared with the harmonics. Unusual and attractive sounds can be obtained by raising and lowering the gong, slowly or quickly (one can even produce a vibrato!) and striking the instrument at appropriate moments. As a variant of the above, deep-sided gongs or tamtams can be floated face down on the water, so that when struck they emit a very deep sound. As large baths are required for water gongs, they naturally are not popular with concert promoters!

Crotales.

The term crotale is of Greek origin, and refers in general to instruments made of two small pieces of metal, wood, bone, or ivory, fastened to the thumb and fingers and beaten together like castanets. Today composers use the term crotale for several different kinds of small cymbal, which vary in shape from that of a Turkish cymbal to small thick inverted brass cups which are really tiny bells. There also seems confusion as to whether they should be played in pairs or singly, whether they are tuned or indefinite in pitch, and certainly there is little evidence as to what pitch limits are normal. Further, crotales are sometimes termed 'antique cymbals', again without any precise indication as to which instruments are intended.

Perhaps it would be best to divide crotales into three specific types: (a) untuned 'finger cymbals', (b) small 'tuned cymbals' of conventional shape, and (c) 'bell crotales', those of cup-like form.

All these instruments have certain factors in common. They are made of brass or bronze alloy comparatively thick for their size, and when struck lightly emit a very pure high sound. They are only suited to very quiet atmospheres and are best flicked with the fingernail or struck lightly with a small wood or metal stick. Excessive force destroys the purity and intonation of the sound without adding much to its volume. In the *Rite of Spring* Stravinsky includes two crotales (played forte together with fortissimo triangle) in a fairly dense context which makes this passage seem more appropriate to the glockenspiel. But his use of two crotales in the quieter concluding section of *Les Noces* is very appropriate. Perhaps the most suggestive use of 'antique cymbals' is in the last bars of Debussy's *L'Après-midi d'un Faune*, where they give the final touch to the work's tenuous sensuality:

Ex. 68   Debussy: *L'Après-midi d'un Faune*

Untuned finger cymbals do not seem to be made in a large variety of sizes. Zildjian makes pairs in two gauges only—thick (highest pitch) and thin. They are fastened to the thumb and index finger by small leather straps or loops.

Finger cymbals can obviously be played fairly rapidly like castanets, but no symphonic score seems to require this, probably because these instruments are most precious to us for their single soft touches. However Britten, in his *War Requiem*, scores a tremolo for antique cymbals, seeming to refer to untuned finger cymbals, as he makes a note that 'if antique cymbals are not available—use untuned pair of small cymbals (clashed) instead'.

Zildjian makes sets of 'metal castanets'—thick 2 in. (5 cm.) diameter finger cymbals (untuned), mounted in pairs on spring steel handles. They can be rapidly played in the intricate rhythms of Latin American music. Such metal castanets have long been a feature of Spanish and Arabic music.

The same firm makes pairs of tuned crotales in the form of small thick cymbals ranging from 2 to 5 in. (5 to 13 cm.) in diameter. Thirteen pairs are available, tuned in a chromatic octave from C in the middle of the treble stave to the C above.[1] For single sounds, a pair of crotales can be played by touching their edges together. But for successions of different sounds, it is preferable to mount an octave of single crotales on a board with special metal supports, in keyboard fashion (diatonic notes in front, chromatic in the rear, in order of pitch). Using appropriate beaters (metal, plastic, or wood) rapid note-successions can then be played. Such a set of crotales is required for the very rapid and complex passages which occur in some modern compositions.

The author has seen a fine set of crotales of Continental make, consisting of circular flat bronze discs of very heavy gauge, hung vertically in a large frame. Twenty-five in number, they covered the entire chromatic range of two octaves upwards from C above middle C.

Even wider pitch ranges have been scored for, but at present it would be most wise to count on modest resources, and write no more than a chromatic octave from C above middle C (sounding an octave higher).

Bell crotales have excellent tone, very silvery and clear. They are to be found (sometimes with internal clappers) in many antique shops in various forms and sizes. Unfortunately, they do not seem to be commercially produced by instrument makers at the time of writing. (See also 'sistrum' for similar tuned bells.)

Musical Saw

At one time this instrument was a common joiner's handsaw, but today this has been replaced by a more finely-tuned steel blade of similar shape, but

---

[1] This is the compass as stated by Zildjian. But they certainly seem to sound an octave higher, and are so indicated in Stockhausen's *Kontakte* and other scores.

without teeth. The blade is fixed to a wooden handle which is held between the knees, while the left hand holds the extremity of the blade.

Sounds are produced either by stroking the edge of the saw with a violin bow, or by striking the blade with a soft stick, such as a felt-headed marimba beater. The bow gives a singing tone, the sound is naturally sustained, and expressive crescendos and diminuendos are easily produced. When the saw is played by striking, there are two separate sounds. The first is a rather unmusical 'clonk' when the blade is struck, and then there follows, at a lower dynamic level, the more 'singing' tone.

It is not easy to play the saw perfectly in tune. As the pitch depends on minute gradations of curvature given to the blade by the left hand, and the exact curvature for a given note cannot easily be judged, the instrument has to be played by ear. It is quite common to hear a note played first out of tune and then rapidly adjusted to the correct pitch. Such pitch adjustments are often hidden behind a fairly pronounced 'vibrato'—a very characteristic feature with this instrument produced by shaking the blade slightly—but any sounds which are initially out of tune are much more evident when the saw is played by striking.

Every movement from one note to another is done by glissando, so that the player can flex the blade correctly for each new sound. The saw is therefore most suited to sustained, singing passages, where vibrato and glissando are not out of place. The music should not move too quickly and staccato passages should be avoided. Given adequate time, the saw can leap over large intervals, but when movement is more rapid, the intervals should be smaller:

Ex. 69

Mayuzumi: *Microcosmos*

Musical Saw

Flexatone

This instrument is a kind of variant of the musical saw. A thin steel blade of somewhat triangular shape is fixed at its base into a metal frame, to which a handle is attached. The free end of the blade is near the handle, so that the blade can be flexed by the thumb of the hand holding the instrument. Slightly curved steel springs are fixed to each side of the blade, with a softwood ball fastened to each free end. When the instrument is shaken, the softwood balls strike the blade, and the intonation can be adjusted with the thumb.

The sound is high-pitched and shrill, but not loud. Single strokes are possible, but a 'tremolo' is more characteristic. The flexing of the blade produces characteristic scooping glissandos, or an exaggerated vibrato.

The flexatone has a wide range of pitch and is not without expressive possibilities, but the actual intonation is so uncertain and variable that it is a mistake to write a part requiring such exactitude of pitch as Schoenberg does in the third variation of his Variations for Orchestra. In any case the flexatone is here completely drowned by the rest of the orchestra.

The instrument is much more suited to musical buffoonery, as in Mauricio Kagel's *Match*. In this piece the serious efforts of two cellists are gradually brought to nothing by the percussion player, whose playing becomes less and less serious, until he brings the piece to an end with a very amusing flexatone solo, at which the cellists give up in despair:

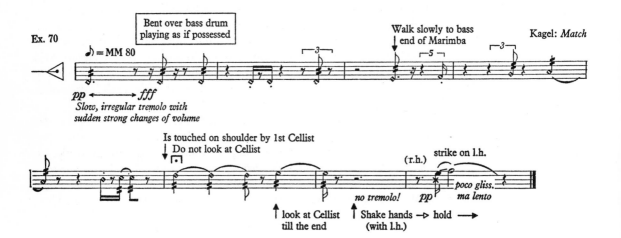

Glasses

It is strange that the expanding tonal spectrum of percussion has not yet led to the exploitation of various types of glass sounds. Alongside the increasing variety of 'wood', 'metal', and 'membrane' sounds could exist yet another—'glass'—but the fashion for glass sounds seems to be dying rather than expanding.

Strangely enough, some electronic music compositions make considerable use of sounds like splintering glass, but only one symphonic composition (Davidson's *Auto Accident*) seems to feature such a sound-effect.

In general, glass may be said to have two different kinds of sounds, those obtained when it is struck, and those produced when it is stroked with damp fingers. Again it would not be far-fetched to say that both kinds of sounds have very similar counterparts in electronic music, but are almost always omitted from percussive music. Yet both kinds of sound were popular enough two and even three hundred years ago. Glasses were tuned by filling them with water for Gluck's famous 'Concerto upon Twenty-six Drinking-Glasses' as long ago as 1746, and glasses were also specially made to give chromatic scales over a wide range.

Sometimes the glasses were struck, but more often they were stroked with a wetted finger, and this latter method was developed into what must have been a fascinating instrument, the glass harmonica, in which a set of tuned glass bowls were rotated by a treadle and sounded by stroking the wetted rims with the fingers. This instrument caused quite a sensation and many composers wrote for it, including Mozart and Beethoven. Its singing, pure tones must have been quite beautiful, yet in modern scores, the sounding of glasses by stroking seems to have disappeared. They are almost always struck, but composers seem to be obstinately indifferent as to the exact pitch and timbre of the sound when writing for this medium. In his *Symphonies de Timbres* Haubenstock-Ramati scores for four glasses ('crystals') designated as soprano, alto, tenor, and bass, but no pitch is given. By 'crystals' he seems to mean very fine crystal tumblers of widely different pitch. The work begins and ends with the glasses featured prominently over a background of double basses, cymbals, and a gong:

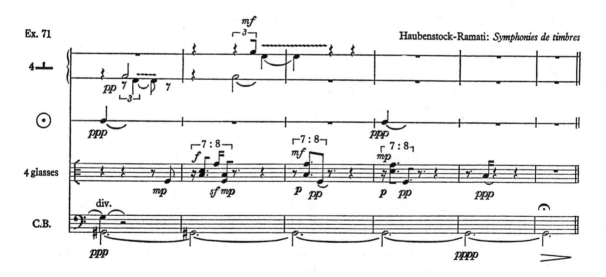

Ex. 71   Haubenstock-Ramati: *Symphonies de timbres*

In his *Concerto for Percussion and Orchestra*, Henry Cowell writes somewhat vaguely for 'five porcelain bowls (not tuned, but of different tone-heights, such as Pyrex bowls, etc.)'. These serve mostly as a kind of ostinato, and together with five untuned 'metal sounds' and four gongs, must provide a most unusual background for the following glockenspiel solo:

In *Reaktionen* for four percussionists, Bo Nilsson includes 'five empty glass bottles' among the instruments for each player, while in *Jeux 6* for six percussion performers, Haubenstock-Ramati specifies 'five glass blocks or flasks'. One feels that these composers are indifferent to the precise sounds which are produced. Perhaps this is in keeping with the imprecise, aleatory music these composers write, in which 'chance' effects are deliberately cultivated.

If glass sounds are ever to be developed on a par with the other three types of percussion sounds, a good deal of research will have to be carried out, and equipment will have to be standardized. Until composers become aware of the possibilities of glass instruments and state their exact requirements, the present state of decadence will continue.

Steel Drums

These instruments have become common in the Antilles, where they are made by cutting off the tops of oil drums and leaving a portion of the side attached so as to form a resonating chamber. A deep side is used for drums intended for accompaniment and a more shallow one for melody instruments.

The drum top is heated and hammered until it is slightly concave. Certain sections are then partly isolated from the rest of the instrument by cutting grooves, and these sections are then tuned to different notes by further hammering.

A 'steel drum' is therefore really not a drum at all, but rather pieces of tuned metal attached to a resonating chamber. When played with soft-headed sticks, these drums produce sounds which are not unlike those of the marimba, but with an added metallic quality. The instruments are usually played by a group of players (a 'steel band'), some playing the melody and others the accompaniment. The drums hang in front of the player, being suspended by cords running over the shoulders and behind the neck.

Sanza

The sanza (sansa or zanza) is a purely African instrument, being found only in Central and South Africa. It consists of a number of thin metal or bamboo blades, flattened at one end, and fastened to a resonating board or flat box. The blades are laid alongside each other in a row (about twelve in number) so that their thinned-down ends project over the edge of a ramp on the resonator. The other ends of the blades are firmly clamped down under a bridge. In this way, the projecting ends of the blades are free to vibrate, so that when plucked they produce a mellow, twanging sound.

Each blade of the sanza emits a different note, tuning being carried out by adjusting the length of the freely-vibrating portion of each individual blade. Sanzas are tuned to the notes of the diatonic or pentatonic scale, and have a compass of up to two octaves.

9 | idiophones of indefinite pitch I—played by striking

METALS—TRIANGLE. CYMBALS. TAMTAM. COWBELLS
ANVIL AND METAL BLOCKS. LUJON. BRONZE SHEETS
STEEL PLATES

WOODS—CLAVES. WOOD BLOCK. TEMPLE BLOCKS. WOOD DRUMS
WHIP OR SLAPSTICK. BAMBOOS OR WOOD CHIMES

GLASS—GLASS CHIMES

The Triangle

This instrument is made from a bar of steel bent into the form of a triangle and left open at one corner, where one end of the bar is sometimes bent into a hook. The instrument is usually held by suspending it with a gut cord looped through one of the closed corners. It may be held in the left hand and beaten with the right, or can be suspended from any convenient support and beaten with either hand, the other being used for damping.

Triangles are usually available in three sizes, 6 in., 8 in. and 10 in. (15, 20 and 25 cm.), but both smaller and larger instruments are available. The triangle emits a profusion of very pure, high sounds of clearly-defined pitch, giving that characteristic brilliant, luminous sound which blends so well with other orchestral instruments. For such a simple instrument, the triangle has an astonishingly full sound-spectrum. An analysis of the sounds emitted by one instrument revealed that there were thirty-nine tones in the range between 700 and 15,500 Hertz, and that no less than thirteen were of prominent volume. The fundamental was one of the weaker tones.

Various beaters may be used. Most common is the metal rod of medium weight, but a wooden drum stick may be indicated for very soft, delicate effects. The wood stick tends to enhance the lowest sound of the triangle and subdue the harmonics, so that a soft mellow tone can be obtained. On the other hand a thin, light metal beater will enhance the upper partials, and produce a light, silvery sound.

Single strokes are usually played on the base of the triangle where the greatest volume can be obtained, but sounds of different quality can be had by striking at other points—an angle, for instance, gives a more silvery sound. The tremolo is performed by rapid strokes between two sides of the bar at the upper angle.

Composers of the last century discovered that a triangle tremolo could add considerable brilliance at the peak of an orchestral fortissimo. However, the best uses of the triangle are in the lower dynamics. A soft stroke, solo, can introduce a moment of innocent purity. Together with soft string or wood-wind chords in upper registers, the triangle can contribute effectively to transparent, scintillating atmospheres without itself being heard too distinctly.

Melodies of a delicate or gay nature, especially for the upper woodwind or strings, can acquire an added brilliance if the triangle joins in with discrimina-tion. If it is beaten rapidly, its volume of sound tends to build up uncontrol-lably, so that it may become too prominent. For the same reason rapid rhythmic figures become confused. Especially in quick passages, it is best if the instrument only 'picks out' the main accents of the melody. In fact one can say that the more sparingly it is used the more effective will be the result:

Due to its penetrating tone it is best to mark the dynamics of the triangle well below those of the instrument it accompanies, as above.

The tremolo, sometimes called a trill or roll, is written thus: ♪ A quiet tremolo with a wooden stick or light metal beater can give brightness to the general orchestral texture but its dynamics must be marked down carefully. A fortissimo tremolo has considerable power, once the instrument has built up its sonority, and can penetrate the loudest orchestral tutti. However, the effect can easily become banal and overworked, and should be reserved only for points of the utmost brilliance. For instance, in *The Planets* Holst only uses the triangle tremolo twice, first in a held tutti chord *fff*, which interrupts the rapid movement in *Jupiter*, then later in the same movement, where there is a rapid ostinato passage in the high strings and woodwind at full volume, against the stabbing brass melody.

Of course the triangle may be damped at any moment after striking, by touching it with the fingers. Some scores indicate that it must be muted or 'muffled' by holding the left hand against the instrument, or even by wrap-ping it tightly in a cloth—surely an extreme measure.

Large triangles are most suitable for fortissimo, smaller instruments for lighter textures. Usually, the player himself is left to decide what size of instrument is most suitable.

Cymbals

For a considerable time orchestral cymbals were always used in pairs, clashed together, but this usage is becoming less common, as single suspended cymbals have a greater variety of effect. The Turkish-type cymbals usually employed in orchestras are circular bronze plates, slightly saucer-shaped, with a central dome or cupola. Chinese cymbals have a turned-up edge, producing a soft oriental tone which has not found much favour in Western music.

Pairs of cymbals are made in various gauges, and can vary in size from 8 to 24 in. (20 to 60 cm.) in diameter. However, those used in orchestras are usually between 17 and 22 in. (44 to 57 cm.) in diameter. Pairs of cymbals are 'matched', so that one cymbal produces higher sounds than the other. There are different ideals in cymbal tone, some countries requiring quite different tonal colours from others. So with paired cymbals, weights or gauges (which govern the tone-colour and attack) fall into three categories: (1) Germanic (or Wagnerian)—heavy cymbals giving a 'clanging' attack, (2) Viennese—medium-heavy, with a 'zing' attack, and (3) French—medium-thin to thin cymbals, with a 'swishing' attack. The medium-heavy gauge is most suited for general use elsewhere.

Pairs of cymbals, held by straps, can be played in three ways:
(a) they may be clashed together with an oblique movement, ending with the cymbals held high in the air after a forte stroke. For soft strokes the edges may be touched together lightly.

If the sounds are to be brief, the cymbals are damped against the chest. Long notes may be indicated 'let ring' or 'L.V.' (*Lasciar vibrare*), or a tie may be written on the note struck, with no note following. In any case exact directions must always be given:

Ex. 74

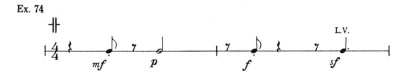

(The use of a pair of cymbals may be indicated by the plural '*piatti*' or by 'a 2').
(b) A two-plate roll may be played by rubbing the plates together with a rapid rotary movement. This roll, a favourite of Wagner, is very uneven in effect, and compared with the brilliance and polish of a two-stick roll on a suspended cymbal is positively uncouth.

(c) One plate may be rapidly swished across the other (sometimes indicated *strisciato*). This gives a hissing, thin metallic ring (without a 'crash') which can be produced in no other way, and is most effective. The slightest whisper is possible.

Suspended cymbals have a hole in the centre of the dome, so that the instrument may be placed on a special pillar stand and screwed into position. Rubber or felt rests prevent the damping of the vibrations. (Formerly, one of a pair of cymbals was held by its strap in the left hand and struck with a stick by the free hand, but as this method is cumbersome and prevents the playing of a roll with two sticks, it is no longer used.)

Single cymbals are made in seven gauges—paper-thin, thin, medium-thin, medium, medium-heavy, heavy, and extra-heavy, and are sold in sizes varying from 8 to 26 in. (20 to 65 cm.) diameter. The medium and heavier gauges are used in concert work, while thinner gauges are preferred by jazz drummers for their stinging, high-pitched ring.

Given the very wide ranges in size manufactured and the various gauges, a considerable variety of cymbal tone is available. But as any good instrument can be made to produce different tones by using a variety of sticks, and by striking it in several ways (e.g. on the rim, near the centre, etc.), there is no need to score for many different sizes.

The sound of a cymbal is a complex of tones ranging from fairly low to very high registers. A soft blow and soft-headed sticks elicit the lower tones, while a hard stroke and hard sticks will bring out the higher ones.

A large cymbal struck gently near the rim with a very soft stick can produce a low sound not unlike a small tamtam. Used gently, a wood snare drum stick on the rim of the same cymbal will make the high overtones predominate, while if it is used forte, the sound is a high-pitched clash. A metal beater in quiet dynamics will produce a narrower band of sounds in the middle register. Sometimes composers indicate the use of a metal beater in loud passages, but this does not produce a satisfactory volume of sound, and there is risk of damaging the cymbal.

Further changes of pitch and colour can be obtained by striking a cymbal away from the rim or even on the central dome. The fullest range of sounds (high, medium, and low) is obtained by a glancing blow one-third in from the rim. From this point, the nearer the centre the cymbal is struck, the more the range of tones narrows down, until at the dome itself only a few medium-pitched sounds predominate. A soft stick on the dome, produces a thin gong-like timbre, while a hard stick gives an empty 'pinging' sound.

The cymbal is therefore the opposite of the tamtam—the fullest tone (comprising low, medium, and high sounds) is produced towards the rim, and not at the centre. A graphic design of cymbal tones can be drawn as follows:

Fig. 5.

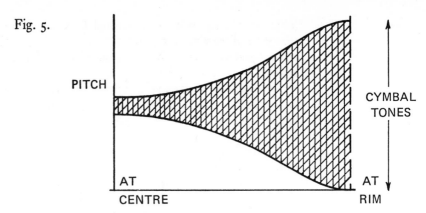

The type of contact sound is important in cymbal playing. A glancing blow with a stick tends to eliminate contact sounds and produce full tone, but a direct stroke produces a hard contact sound and a thinner tone. Heavy cymbals exaggerate contact sounds, but with thin cymbals these are much less evident. Strangely enough, contact sounds are cultivated in jazz (where thin cymbals are used), but are not favoured so much in the symphonic field (where heavier cymbals are mostly employed).

For a particularly full-toned crash, some players use two sticks—one hard, the other soft—so that the full scale of sounds is produced. Alternatively, two cymbals of different sizes can be struck.

The *tremolo* or *roll* is usually played on the suspended cymbal with two soft-headed sticks, and is indicated thus: ♯. A wide dynamic range is possible, with crescendos and diminuendos, but as a gradual build-up of tone is most effective and more in the nature of the instrument, it is preferable to begin a tremolo with a crescendo rather than vice versa.

A suspended cymbal is damped with the fingers of the free hand. This gives great control of the duration of the cymbal's sound and the loudest clash can be instantaneously 'choked'.

The fingers can also be used to mute the instrument. This gives softer, 'dead'-sounding tones which, in combination with undamped sounds, have been greatly exploited by jazz drummers in 'ride' cymbal work:

Ex. 75

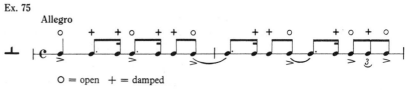

O = open + = damped

This contrast of ringing and 'dead' cymbal tone is most effective, but is rarely used in concert music.

In some scores a large number of cymbals are used to form a fluctuating background 'metal' colour. For example, in Nono's *Cori di Didone*, the only accompaniment to the choir is eight cymbals, four tamtams, and bells. These are used with rapid alternations of staccato, tremolos, sforzandos, and big dynamic changes, so that there is a rapid interplay of timbres, rather than the spread of special colours over wide areas:

Ex. 76

Luigi Nono: *Cori de Didone*

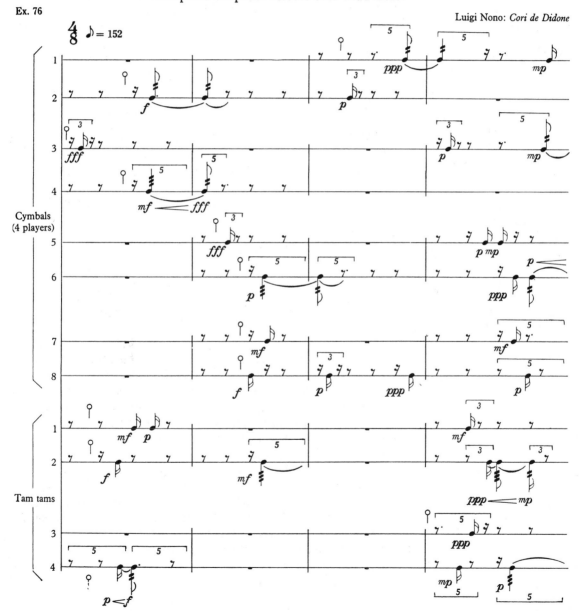

As the instruments are only played with either soft beaters or wire brushes, and there is no indication of sounds played at the centre or near the rim, it would seem that in spite of using many instruments, their full colouristic possibilities have not been exploited.

The *duration* of all cymbal sounds (whether rolled or not) should be very exactly indicated. Performers complain that some composers (one example is Mahler) often indicate all cymbal sounds by a crotchet, so that they have to discover during rehearsals whether the notes should be choked, or just how long they should be allowed to ring.

Wire brushes are particularly effective for quiet cymbal strokes, and if the brush is held against the cymbal after it is struck, a prolonged tingling sound can be produced.

The whole catalogue of cymbal effects is too extensive to give in detail, for composers have called not only for the use of every available beater in the percussionist's outfit, but have indicated all kinds of bizarre practices. These range from brushing the cymbal with a silver coin or hitting it with a triangle, to scraping it with a saw-edge or screw rod and playing a tremolo on the cymbal with a cello bow.

Two jazz cymbals could be put to good use in orchestral music: the 'sizzle' cymbal and the 'hi-hat' or 'foot' cymbals:

The *sizzle cymbal* is usually a large (18 to 22 in. (46 to 56 cm.)) thin cymbal with holes bored near the rim, in which are inserted loose rivets. When the cymbal is struck, the rivets rattle as long as the instrument continues to vibrate, producing a sizzling, high-pitched sound. This gives single strokes a longer sound-duration than with a normal cymbal, while rolls have a more uniform ring. A sizzle cymbal is sometimes made by fastening several pins on to a thread, which is laid over the plate.

Hi-hat cymbals are made of a pair of cymbals, one fastened on top of a vertical tube, the other fixed to a rod which runs inside the tube. A foot pedal attached to the rod allows one plate to be clashed against the other, and on releasing the pressure, the plates are separated by the action of a spring. The top cymbal should be pitched higher than the lower one to give a 'blended' tone. Hi-hat cymbals work in principle like two cymbals clashed together, but the volume is considerably less, and as the plates are 'choked' by their own contact, there is less ring after the clash.

In concert music, foot cymbals are occasionally used so as to allow the performer greater liberty while playing other instruments with both hands. By adequate foot control it is possible to obtain two main effects. If the plates are clashed and then held together, a sharp 'click' is produced, but if the plates are immediately separated this gives a 'splashing' sound.

Jazz drummers play effective rhythmic patterns on the hi-hat with side drum sticks, with or without simultaneous use of the foot pedal. For stick work, the cymbals are usually kept in a position where they barely touch each other. The sticks can play on the top of the upper cymbal or at the edge, while a heavier, full-bodied sound can be obtained by using the shoulder of a stick on the rim.

An interesting effect is to play underneath the bottom cymbal with the left stick and use the right stick on the top cymbal. The thumb and first finger of the left hand control the ring and tone of the cymbals by damping or releasing. The plates may be played either in closed or semi-open position to give a variety of tonal effects, while the stick work can be as intricate and complex as side-drum playing. Good hi-hat playing can in this way contribute a great deal to the overall sound and rhythmic effectiveness. Unfortunately hi-hat playing is so typically 'jazz' that it would be difficult to insert it into symphonic usage without detriment to the aesthetic effect.

Tamtam

The term 'tamtam' is often indiscriminately used to indicate either some types of gong, or gongs in general. On the other hand, the term 'gong' is often used when tamtams seem to be referred to. Many authorities of note seem to regard tamtams and gongs as being identical, and even percussion instrument catalogues do not always make a clear differentiation between these instruments.

It is therefore perhaps wrong to insist too much on the difference between these instruments. Yet their sounds are different enough, and this is surely the important issue, and must dictate a difference in terminology.

The truth is that 'gongs' is the correct term for the whole family of instruments which includes both gongs and what have come to be known as 'tamtams'. Yet ever since about 1790, the term 'tamtam' has been used in Europe and has gradually acquired a precise significance, meaning a type of gong which emits sounds of indefinite pitch.

Tamtams are large bronze alloy discs which are usually made of thinner material than gongs. They are usually flat or slightly saucer-shaped and the rim is shallow, often only slightly rounded. The centre has no boss or protuberance. The usual shapes to be found are as follows:

Fig. 6.

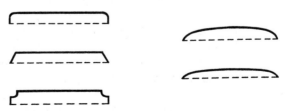

Apart from the different shape, the main distinguishing feature of the tamtam is its sound. Because of its thinner gauge, the instrument emits much more high-pitched overtones than the gong, overtones which tend towards the confused shrillness which characterizes the cymbal. In fact the sound of a small tamtam is much more similar to that of a large heavy-weight cymbal than to the harmonious resonance of a well-tuned gong.

Tamtam sounds comprise a very large number of tones, extending from a low fundamental note to high, shimmering overtones. It is possible to separate these off to some extent, so that a fair variety of sounds can be produced from one instrument.

A deep clear sound can be brought out by striking a tamtam softly at the centre with a soft, heavy beater. But as soon as force is used, or a harder beater, those shrill, discordant overtones will be added which cause tamtams to be included in the category of instruments of indefinite pitch.

When struck at the rim, a splash of high overtones is produced, with a harsh discordant effect.

If the fullest sound is required from a tamtam, comprising all its sounds in balanced proportion, the instrument should be struck at a point which is just off centre. Large instruments will only give out their full sounds with a succession of beats, giving the effect of a gradual crescendo. Repeated beats are essential for fortissimo.

In general, soft beaters cause deep sounds to predominate, while hard beaters bring out the higher tones. Wooden or metal beaters produce a prominent 'contact' sound or 'ping', in addition to the normal clashing harmonics.

Tamtams for orchestral use are made in sizes ranging from about 18 in. (46 cm.) diameter up to 36 in. (91 cm.) or more.[1] They are hung from a circular steel support and are provided with a heavy wooden mallet covered with lamb's wool. Like gongs, they may also be played with timpani sticks, side drum sticks, or triangle beaters, these latter producing more brilliant sounds. As mentioned above, these harsher sounds can be brought out more forcefully if the instrument is struck near or at the rim (see Stockhausen's *Kontakte* p. 27 etc. for the production of various timbres).

Repeated strokes build up a thrilling crescendo without the repetition of beats being over-evident. In fact with large instruments the repetition of strokes will not be heard at all.

A quiet tremolo gives a shimmering luminosity to orchestral harmonies (see Ex. 77).

One of the most useful effects of the tamtam is the way it can 'clinch' a climax with a fortissimo stroke and then, as its vibrations die, introduce a tranquil atmosphere in complete contrast. No other instrument can so effectively fuse 'war' and 'peace' together (see Ex. 78).

[1] M.M. Paiste & Sohn make tamtams from 7 in. (18 cm.) up to 60 in. (150 cm.) diameter.

Ex. 77   Presto ♩. = 100   Schoenberg: *Film Music Op. 34*

Ex. 78   Brindle: *Homage to H. G. Wells*

Composers often use soft strokes on tamtams of different sizes in music of a tenuous nature. Particularly in 'pointilliste' orchestration (where sounds are passed from one instrument to another in a rather fragmentary manner) the soft vibrations of the tamtams provide a sound substratum on which other instrumental sounds can be laid, without their sparseness seeming too thin and naked.

A harsh, ringing sound can be produced by running a metal triangle beater round a tamtam rim. The rim is usually uneven, with corrugations made by hammering the metal. However, the corrugations are so spaced that the beater must be moved quickly to produce an even sound. The result is that this effect cannot be done quietly over a prolonged period, but at forte, it may be sustained for as long as necessary.

Damping of the tamtam can be done from the centre (eliminating the deeper tones first) or from the rim (with the opposite effect). The exact duration of the sound should be indicated, as the instrument's vibrations last some time.

Cowbells

Particularly on the Continent, these may be authentic herd cowbells made in bronze alloy with an oval form, and a 'frog-mouth' shape at the open end. The clapper is usually removed and the bells hung by leather thongs. They may vary in size from 3 in. (7 cm.) to about 10 in. (25 cm.) overall, though large ones are rarely used. Cowbells (or 'cencerros') made by instrument manufacturers have a more triangular form and are bronze or chromium-plated. They are usually made in rigidly mounted sets of two, three, or four, though it is possible to make a choice of five or six ranging between 3 and 7½ in. (7 and 19 cm.) in size and with consequent pitch variety.

Cowbells are usually played with a snare drum stick, the sound being hard and clanky, tending to die quickly. The pitch oscillates considerably due to the deformation of the instrument, particularly when they are struck hard, so cowbells must not normally be regarded as tuned percussion. Their pitch does not vary greatly with their size, so if well-contrasting sounds are required it is best to use cowbells of widely differing dimensions.

They have occasionally been used in symphonic music to evoke an Alpine atmosphere (as in Mahler's Sixth Symphony), but by far their greatest use is to be found in African and Latin American music. Sometimes a cowbell is used as a rhythmic ostinato throughout an entire dance, as in the 'mambo':

Ex. 79

Mambo

Through the influence of Latin American music, cowbells are frequently featured in jazz, but in serious music they have been neglected. However, *avant-garde* composers are beginning to use these instruments in both tuned and untuned forms to a fair degree.

Perhaps their most effective use is in Berio's *Tempi Concertati*, where they are combined with wood blocks, bongos, and tomtoms in a truly virtuoso gesture:

Ex. 80

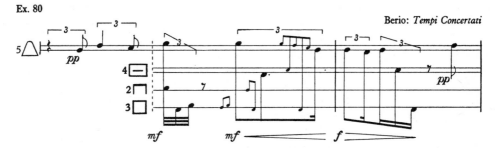

Berio: *Tempi Concertati*

Cowbells may be muted or 'muffled' by inserting a handkerchief or piece of cloth into the aperture. This deadens the ring. They may also be played with soft felt-headed sticks to give a mellower tone.

Recently experiments have been made in tuning genuine herd bells and sets of instruments have been made with a chromatic compass of two and a half octaves from F below middle C to *c'''* two octaves above middle C. These sets of herd bells are intended to be played with soft-headed sticks, so as to produce a hollow, mellow sound which is not obtainable with other tuned percussion instruments. However, at the moment there are very few scores indeed which call for such sets of tuned herd bells—the most prominent examples are Messiaen's *Et Expecto Resurrectionem Mortuorum*, Stockhausen's *Gruppen* and a number of pieces written specially for the Strasbourg 'Groupe Instrumental à Percussion'.

Anvil or Metal Blocks

Anvils have been used in opera scores, both on and off the stage, for realistic purposes. Wagner's *Rheingold* includes eighteen in the score, in three different sizes. They have been occasionally included in modern scores such as Bloch's *America* to give 'industrial atmosphere', while a few scores give them a role which is exclusively musical (e.g. Lukas Foss's *Echoi*).

An anvil may be made in various forms. It may be a round bar or rectangular block of steel suspended by a cord and struck with a hammer, or such pieces of steel may be laid on a pad of soft felt if this does not over-impede the metal's vibration. In *Ionisation* Varèse describes precisely what is required—a 2½ in. (6 cm.) tube 8 to 10 in. (20 to 25 cm.) long and a 1¾ in. (4.5 cm.) tube

9 in. (23 cm.) long are laid on soft felt and fit in half-round channels in a wood block. These tubes are beaten with a piece of thinner tubing, either separately, or together (by holding the beating tube in the middle). The anvils are reserved exclusively for loud passages, and play fairly rapid rhythms:

In *La Vierge, le Vivace et le Bel Aujourd'hui*, Boulez uses two metal blocks which are played with soft xylophone beaters. The type of block is not specified. The dynamic scale is generally between pianissimo and a maximum of mezzo-forte. The blocks are played almost continuously in the main sections of this piece, and the composer's intention is obviously to produce soft mellow metallic sounds of indefinite pitch, rather than the 'clanking of anvils'. (The voice part, in fact, is accompanied throughout by metal instruments of one kind and another—vibraphones, bells, metal blocks, tamtams, crotales, cymbals, and gongs. The non-metallic sounds—harp and drums—have a secondary role.)

The metal blocks have a part which is full of movement and abundant in dynamic nuances:

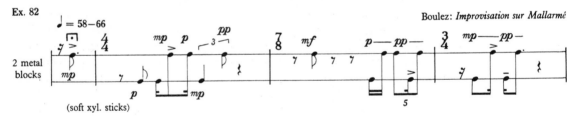

Ross Lee Finney specifies an 'anvil with the pitch of F' in his Symphony No. 2 at a point where the instrument must be in tune with the rest of the orchestra. But though real anvils have been made with definite pitches for opera music of the last century, we can hardly count on their being readily available now. It seems most sensible to write for an instrument of indefinite pitch and to give a fair indication of its construction. We must at least give the performer enough information for him to decide whether to hit a real anvil with a heavy hammer, or to give a small metal block a soft blow with a rubber mallet.

Ludwig of Chicago makes a small anvil consisting of a solid steel bar resting in two padded supports, and a special steel mallet is provided. Some players use steel brake drums as anvils, and the results are quite satisfactory.

Lujon

This instrument is made from six large squares of metal, with resonators below, fixed in a rectangular frame. Alternatively, the metal squares may be fixed as tongues in the top of a tall resonating box. The sounds are untuned but are mellow in quality, with a characteristic resonant 'boom', not unlike the lowest notes of the marimba and vibraphone. Berio uses the lujon effectively in *Circles* as a lower (untuned) extension of the vibraphone.

Bronze Sheets

Thin bronze sheets about five feet long and 24 in. wide are occasionally used for loud effects. The sheet may be shaken or buckled to give out sounds like highly-pitched thunder cracks, or it may be suspended and struck with a wooden mallet or steel hammer. Alternatively, a crackling sound can be obtained by running a steel chain over an edge of the sheet.

Luigi Nono uses six bronze sheets in his *A Floresta é Jovem e Chea de Vida*, for live performers and pre-recorded sounds. His intention is obviously to obtain crashes of overpowering volume, but unfortunately the noise produced from the sheets seems thin and ineffective compared with the thunder of the electronically reproduced sounds. On the other hand, in Cage's *Construction in Metal*, the volume scale is such that bronze sheets build up the peaks of intensity.

Steel Plates

Very rarely, composers have included steel plates or sheets in their scores, to be struck with steel hammers. Obviously their intention is to produce a very powerful crash, but there is a probability that their intentions may not be realized. For until there is adequate information as to the size, thickness, shape, and quality of the steel plate which is most suited for a specific sound, there can be no guarantee that the result will be anything like that which the composer intended. In any case the composer's conception of such sounds is quite personal, and unless he supervises the selection of materials himself, he is bound to be disappointed.

Steel or bronze plates have been specially made to produce relatively low sounds of definite pitch and their sound is mellow when the volume is not forced. There are certainly possibilities for development in this field. Bronze plates have long been a feature of Oriental music.

Claves

Claves are nothing other than two pieces of wood beaten against each other. The most common types are the Cuban and oriental claves. Cuban claves are round pieces of pao-pao, iron wood, or Mexican rosewood, and vary from

7 to 8 in. (17 to 20 cm.) in length. As the most characteristic sound is high and penetrating, claves should be of very hard wood and not too large. They are usually played by holding one clave loosely with the left fingers high above the palm of the hand (thus forming a hollow resonator), and beating it at the middle with the other clave held between the right thumb and forefinger.

Oriental claves are six-sided, and are beaten against each other when held in the form of an 'X'.

The pitch of claves is higher than temple blocks or wood blocks, and the sound is much more penetrating. They have been mostly used in playing simple ostinato patterns. For instance Chavez's *Toccata* for percussion has the following design:

Ex. 83   Chávez: *Toccata*

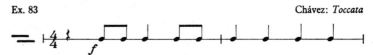

The two following ostinatos are used in Latin American dances:

Ex. 84

Rumba

Bossa Nova

Apart from such ostinato figurations, composers have not attempted much of interest. Boulez uses three sizes of claves in *Une Dentelle s'Abolit* from the *Improvisation sur Mallarmé*, each pair played by a different player. But their use is limited only to one effect. The claves play isolated sounds together, fortissimo, while other instruments hold a loud chord. The effect is dramatic, but could be easily overworked.

Varèse seems to favour rapid rhythms in *Ionisation*:

Ex. 85   Varèse: *Ionisation*

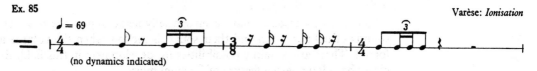

but like others, he tends mostly towards the ostinato.

Wood Blocks

Wood blocks, sometimes called 'Chinese' blocks, are usually made of thick rectangular blocks of hardwood 6½ to 8 in. (16 to 20 cm.) long. Long slots are cut longitudinally near the top and bottom so as to provide hard, thin wood surfaces which produce highly resonant sounds. They are played in a horizontal position, and beaten on the top surface.

Blocks are usually made in two or three sizes to give sounds of different pitch, though Ludwig makes an ebonite model which can be tuned to different pitches. Some firms make a 'two-tone' hollow tubular block supported in the middle with slots at each end which give different pitches.

Small knuckle-shaped blocks imported from Hong Kong are ideal for high-pitched sounds.

The sound should be crisp and clear, but it has a certain hollowness which is not found in claves. Wood blocks are usually midway in pitch between temple blocks and claves. They are sometimes used with temple blocks to continue the sounds of the latter into a higher register, and as the tone of the two kinds of instrument is similar (though temple blocks have a more hollow sound), they combine very well.

Wood blocks are usually played with side drum sticks and any rhythms suitable for drums can be played equally well on the blocks. The tremolo is particularly effective.

Unfortunately, the wood block is sometimes associated in our minds with a particularly outmoded kind of traditional jazz playing. But one has only to hear the poetic and dramatic atmosphere such instruments can evoke in Chinese theatre music to realize that the family of wood and temple blocks has expressive potentialities of no mean order.

Varèse writes a dramatic part for two wood blocks in *Hyperprism*, where they give an exciting chattering background to the agitated piccolo and E flat clarinet:

Ex. 86   Varèse: *Hyperprism*

The following passage for three wood blocks shows the various effects possible. Note the 'crushed' notes, (particularly effective before a single loud note as at 'a'), rapid reiterations, the tremolo, the sforzando 'chord' on two blocks, and the wide range of dynamics:

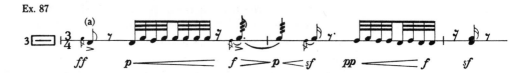

Ex. 87

Wood block passage work can be effectively combined with other instruments, particularly temple blocks, cowbells, log drum, and so on. In Berio's *Circles*, wood blocks are even played with the marimba to give some very effective embellishments:

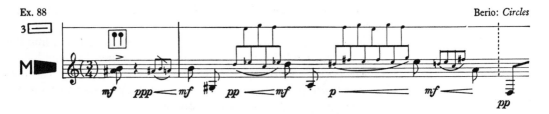

Ex. 88   Berio: *Circles*

Wood blocks can be muted (or 'muffled', to give the American term) by either damping the beaten surface with one hand or laying a cloth over it, so that two sticks can be used.

Temple Blocks

These are sometimes referred to as 'Chinese' or 'Korean' temple blocks—which would be more correct if their origins are considered important. But as there seems some risk of confusion between wood blocks and temple blocks if both are referred to as 'Chinese blocks' (this sometimes happens—in fact in some scores it is difficult to guess which is required), it seems best to omit the term 'Chinese' in both cases.

Temple blocks are usually made in sets of five supported on a special stand with three blocks below and two above. They are rounded or oval in form, carved from hardwood, and completely hollowed out inside. There is a wide mouth-like slit from 'ear to ear', in fact some blocks have a 'dragon's-head' shape and are painted with an oriental dragon-like motif. They vary in size according to pitch and are not infrequently tuned to the pentatonic scale—though they should not normally be used as pitched instruments.

Temple blocks have a deeper, more hollow tone than wood blocks, and the sound is more sustained, due to the larger resonating chamber. To illustrate the sound, one might say that if claves 'click' and the wood block 'clacks', then temple blocks 'clock'. In fact the sound is not unlike the clacking of the tongue if the mouth is well open. However, the tone changes according to the sticks used. Temple blocks are usually sold with two soft-headed mallets with cane handles and these give a mellow subdued tone of almost 'melodious' character. But if snare drum sticks are used the tone is brighter and dryer, combining well with wood block sounds.

Especially with side drum sticks—which give a superior 'bounce'—temple blocks can be used with all the flams, ruffs, rolls, and rapidly reiterated notes of drum technique, while 'passage work' over the blocks is particularly effective:

Ex. 89

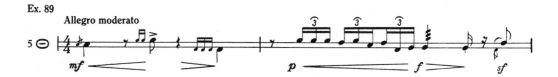

Composers have occasionally indicated a glissando over the blocks, obviously more effective if all the blocks are in line, but still possible with the blocks in the usual two rows, if two sticks are used.

Temple blocks are hardly suited to continuous use, and should obviously be reserved for special effects.

The *mokubio* is an extra large type of temple block, made in the orient. These instruments are usually elaborately carved with dragon-head or oriental-mask motifs, and are available in various sizes. Mokubios have a deep, mellow sound. They should only be played with soft-headed sticks, as they speak slowly, and do not respond well to hard beaters. In fact hard sticks only produce a knocking contact sound without eliciting the mokubio's true tones. They are sometimes termed Buddhist 'slit drums'.

Wood Drums

Though wood drums are spread over several continents, they are only too scarce in our own concert halls. So it seems most practical to mention only those kinds used in modern scores—the log drum and slit drum—and the 'wood-plate drum' (*Holzplattentrommel*), which is a modern attempt to produce something similar in Europe.

The *log drum* (sometimes called the 'wooden gong') is cylindrical in shape and is found in various sizes up to several feet long. The hollow internal cavity is sealed off at each end with wooden stoppers or plates, but an opening is left along the length of the cylinder surface, usually in the form of a slot. The drum is beaten at this point with wooden beaters and usually different tones are obtained by making the wood lips of the slot vary in thickness. Alternatively, different tones are obtained by cutting the wood into two different-sized 'tongues'. Some log drums are not cylindrical, but are made in the form of a trough. The edges of the trough are beaten, and again, different tones can be obtained. Alberto Ginastera scores for six variously sized log drums in *Cantata para America Magica*.

The *slit drum* is shaped like a decked boat with cut-off stem and stern. The top is flat with two wide slots in line, communicating with the internal cavity. The wooden edges of one slot are made thicker than those of the other, so that when struck, different tones are produced. Stockhausen scores for a number of slit drums in several works (two in *Kontakte* and *Zyklus*, six in *Gruppen*). Special tunings are given in *Gruppen* within the compass of an octave and a sixth from F below middle C to the D a ninth above middle C. The two tones on each drum are given as a tritone in all cases. Their chief characteristic is a taut hollow sound of very precise pitch which is quite unlike the more 'tubby' sound of most skin drums. In *Kontakte*, as well as writing for slit drums alone, Stockhausen combines them with marimba sounds and with various cymbal tones. Though the composer specifies the pitch of two tones required on each drum, a simple line notation is used to show which slot has to be struck:

Ex. 90   Stockhausen: *Kontakte*

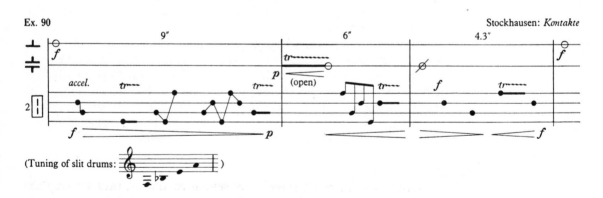

The author has seen slit drums made by nailing plywood round two circular pieces of wood, which form the ends of each drum. A slot is left from end to end of the drum, for the emission of the sound. However, the tone of these instruments is disappointing, and inferior to that of authentic slit drums.

In Europe, modern *wood-plate drums* have been made by glueing thin wooden heads about $\frac{3}{8}$ in. (5 mm.) thick into the tops of tomtom shells to form single-headed drums without any tensioning screws. This kind of drum was used in Puccini's *Turandot*, but fell into disuse until recently, when it was revived in Germany in such modern scores as Stockhausen's *Kontakte*.

This wood-plate drum has little similarity in tone to the slit drum or log drum. The sounds are high-pitched, very crisp and well defined and without the hollowness of tone of the slit drum, or the tubby quality of skin drums. The sound is very attractive and could be used with advantage for decisive, brisk, percussive effects.

Large, hollow bamboos are used in occasional scores of an exotic type. Such instruments have been long used by other cultures. In Java, the Anklung is made of several bamboo tubes fixed vertically in a frame, each tube being tuned by cutting the end diagonally so as to form a long tongue.

Whip or Slapstick

The slapstick is made of two strips of thin hardwood about 2½ in. (6 cm.) wide, and 18 in. (46 cm.) long. They are fastened together with a hinge, and at this point one strip is extended to form a handle. A strong spring keeps the two pieces of wood apart. When the slapstick is swung hard and suddenly arrested, the two hardwood strips strike each other with a whip-like crack.

In the orchestra, the whip is mostly used in loud passages to reinforce staccato orchestral rhythms, or it may be used solo (or with another percussion instrument) in prominent moments of silence in opposition to the rest of the orchestra:

Ex. 91   Aaron Copland: *Rodeo*

However, the whip is capable of quiet dynamics, or a gradual crescendo and diminuendo (by beating the instrument against the knee, or manipulating the wood strips with the hands), so its use could become more extended than at present.

Bamboos or Wood Chimes

A fair number of different-sized hollow bamboo canes are suspended together, sometimes in line, sometimes in a circle. Wood chimes are usually hand made in Africa and the orient. When struck by the hand or stroked with a wooden stick they emit a dry hollow sound and then continue to jangle against each other in a rustling murmur. When grasped suddenly together, they emit a resounding 'chock'. This action is the first indicated in the following quotation from Bruno Maderna's Concerto for Oboe and Chamber Ensemble. The remaining signs suggest various strokes across the bamboos without providing very definite playing indications:

Ex. 92   Maderna: *Oboe Concerto*

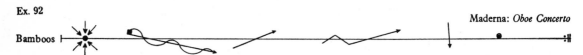

Wood chimes, or 'wind chimes' (as they are sometimes called), have only a small volume, and are most suited to quiet passages. Some composers use them as an upward (untuned) extension of the xylophone or marimba (as in Ex. 26).

The instrument may also be constructed with round bars of thin resonant hardwood of different lengths. These produce a more brittle sound than bamboo canes.

Glass Chimes

These are similar to wood chimes, being various untuned lozenge shapes of glass hung together. They are often suspended from a circular plastic frame. When stroked or shaken, the chimes emit a high-pitched tinkling sound which continues until the movement of the glasses is checked. The volume is small, but the sound makes an attractive background where a hard, shining atmosphere is needed in pianissimo passages.

Glass chimes are occasionally used as an upward (untuned) extension of the glockenspiel, or to add an extra quality to the sound of triangles.

10 | *idiophones of indefinite pitch II—played by shaking, stroking and scraping*

METALS—SISTRUM. SLEIGH BELLS. WASHBOARD

WOODS, ETC.—CASTANETS. MARACAS. CABACA. MEXICAN BEAN
CHOCOLO. GUIRO. RECO-RECO. JAW BONE. RATTLE. CUICA
SAND BLOCKS. SWITCH. THUNDER EFFECTS. WIND MACHINE

Sistrum

The sistrum has taken many forms during its long history, and is still wide-spread in one form or another. But only two types need be considered, and even these are rarely used in orchestral music. The simpler is the sistrum consisting of a frame which holds a number of loose wooden discs strung on a wire or rod. When shaken sharply, these emit a loud clatter. If they are stroked, the sound has a quieter, more rustling quality. This form of instrument is sometimes used in orchestral music which evokes an Eastern atmosphere, or by Latin American symphonic composers (e.g. Ginastera's *Cantata para America Magica*). The Orff-Schulwerk includes a 'jingles rattle' which is really a sistrum. It comprises a cane frame with a long handle, holding four pairs of small metal plates. When shaken, the instrument emits a sound like the jingle of a tambourine, but with a more delicate ring.

A more developed sistrum is made with small cup-shaped metal bells. These are tuned and arranged in order of pitch on two metal bars, diatonic notes on the left, chromatic on the right. The two bars are joined to a wooden handle. The left hand holds the instrument in front of the player while the bells are struck with a small metal-headed beater held in the right hand. This sistrum is therefore not unlike the bell lyra in form, though the latter has a much fuller tone, being virtually a glockenspiel. This sistrum has a compass of about two octaves beginning on G above middle C, though the upper octave may not be fully chromatic. However, the inconvenience of playing this kind of sistrum (with one hand always immobilized) has brought about the use of keyboard sistrums, sometimes called 'celestettes', which have a very pure and gentle tone. The compass is about two octaves from middle C upwards.

The 'Chinese bell-tree' is similar to the tuned sistrum mentioned above, but the cup-shaped bells, though emitting tuned sounds, are arranged on a vertical rod in a haphazard order of pitch. When stroked with small metal beaters, they emit a jangle which can range from piano to a strident forte.

Sleigh Bells

These are made of hollow round metal bells up to about an inch in diameter, with a loose steel ball inside each. They are often fastened, in different sizes and in sets of about ten, to a leather strap. When the strap is shaken the bells jingle with sounds of different pitch. Orchestral models usually have the bells fixed to a long steel frame fastened to a wooden handle. The number of bells may vary from about ten to twenty-five. The advantage of this type is that more precise rhythms may be obtained by striking the frame against the free hand, while an effective tremolo may be produced by agitating the instrument rapidly.

Ever since Cherubini introduced these bells into the orchestra in his opera *Elise* (1794) they have been used to imitate the jingle of mule or horse harness-bells. But occasionally they are used with less realistic intent, simply to give a bright, festive atmosphere (cf. Massenet's *Manon*, Mahler's Fourth Symphony, Respighi's *Feste Romane*, etc.).

Varèse uses sleigh bells in purely abstract music (*Hyperprism*, *Ionisation*, and *Integrales*) to perform precise staccato rhythmic designs (usually of a simple nature) or tremolo. The dynamic range is wide, from piano to fortissimo. In *Kontakte*, Stockhausen uses two sets of sleigh bells (which he terms 'Indian bells') played by the percussionist and pianist in opposition to electronic sounds. Both tremolos and staccato sounds are indicated:

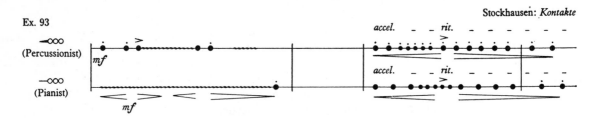

Stockhausen: *Kontakte*

Ex. 93

African dancers often have similar instruments strapped round their wrists and ankles so as to reproduce the rhythm of their movements in an audible form. Such small wrist bells are made also for orchestral use, so that a player may make them jingle as he plays another instrument such as a tambourine.

Washboard

The American Negro slaves used instruments made with a set of bamboo canes laid flat and stroked with a stick, but in the first jazz groups these were replaced by washboards made out of corrugated zinc. The washboard became a characteristic part of the New Orleans band rhythm sections, and with the banjo contributed to the bright, brittle sound of early jazz music.

The instrument is usually laid flat in front of the player on a low table, or on special supports, and he plays with metal thimbles on the fingers of each hand. The traditional way of playing is to stroke the left fingers rapidly backwards and forwards over the corrugations in the characteristic 'eight in a bar' rhythm, while the right hand plays independent rhythms.

Some players can produce effects of considerable virtuosity, in fact good washboard solos can be brilliant exhibitions of musicianship. But the characteristic 'Dixieland' sound of the instrument has inhibited serious composers from using it. However, once this inhibition is overcome, there is no reason why the washboard could not be put to effective use, for it is a remarkably versatile instrument, much more so than would at first appear.

Castanets

These instruments, long associated with Spanish folk music, are made of two hollowed-out, saucer-shaped pieces of ebony or rosewood. The upper portions have projecting ears with holes, through which passes an ornamental string, holding the two castanets together. The string is wound round the thumb, leaving the fingers free to strike the castanets which lie in the palm of the hand. In each pair, one castanet is usually pitched higher than the other.

Two pairs may be used, one pair generally pitched higher than the other, one pair in each hand. This is the traditional mode of playing in Spanish music, where players exhibit great skill in evoking a variety of poetic effects from such simple instruments.

However, this virtuosity cannot usually be expected from orchestral players, and many alternative kinds of castanets have been produced in an effort to find a more practical and easily-played form of instrument. Orchestral instruments may take the form of a pair of castanets fastened one on each side of a hardwood clapper with a long handle, or there may be one pair at each end of the handle. One model has two pairs together at the same end of the handle. Another type, called 'concert castanets' has two bakelite castanets mounted with springs on a hardwood resonating block. These may be played with the fingers or struck with soft mallets.

None of these orchestral models can equal the tonal variety, precision, and vitality of authentic instruments, nor can the exact kind of trill be reproduced.

The conventional Spanish rhythms—e.g. the bolero or fandango—are familiar enough, and music such as the following for castanets is obviously influenced by such associations:

Ex. 94   Milhaud: *Concerto for Percussion*

Composers often use such rhythms in ostinatos to evoke a vivacious atmosphere (e.g. 'Bransle Gay' in Stravinsky's *Agon*, or Britten's *The Young Person's Guide to the Orchestra*) but sometimes the rattle of the castanets is put to more sinister use, as in Walton's *Belshazzar's Feast* at the moment when the King of Babylon sees the hand appear and write on the wall. Considerable rhythmic variety is given to these instruments in Varèse's *Ionisation* and *Intégrales*, though the latter avoids Spanish-type rhythms more than the former.

It seems that if these instruments are to be used in absolute music without risk of bringing out 'folk' associations, anything which resembles Spanish rhythms must be avoided, and it would perhaps be better to reserve their use to darker atmospheres rather than gay ones.

For metal castanets, see 'crotales'.

Maracas

These instruments, which form the rhythmic basis of Latin American music, are among the oldest provided by nature. They were originally made of gourds dried in the sun and emptied. The dried seeds were then put back inside, so that when the gourd was shaken the movement of the seeds produced a dry, rattling sound. At some stage, handles were fixed to the gourds, and the first maracas were complete. They are usually imported from South America or Mexico, and may be true gourds or coconut shells, but mass production has made hardwood models most common, either hand carved or machine turned. Commercial models usually contain lead shot, more authentic instruments dried corn, or pea seeds.

Though they are made in various sizes, they are usually made in pairs of similar size, balanced in pitch, so any variation from this norm should be specifically noted.

The best maracas will give a fairly continuous roll when gently agitated, producing a clear, high-pitched, swishing sound, while a sharp movement of the wrist will produce a clean, hard staccato.

Latin American rhythms for maracas are usually as follows:

Ex. 95

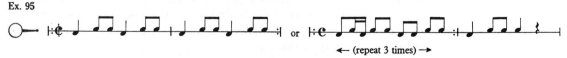

← (repeat 3 times) →

Obviously, symphonic writers will probably keep away from such typical rhythms if they wish to avoid Latin American effects—though Chavez adopts very similar patterns in his *Toccata for Percussion*. Varèse has quite a variety of 'non exotic' rhythms for two maracas of different sizes in *Ionisation*, though behind the rhythmic variety there seems to run a tendency towards the creation of ostinato patterns.

Ex. 96

Varèse: *Ionisation*

One of the most useful functions of the maracas is to provide a quiet roll as a background sound to music of a tenuous nature. The dry roll of the maracas is accentuated by the addition of the sand block in Berio's *Circles* as a background to a quiet harp solo. In *Une Dentelle s'Abolit*, Boulez has three maracas players playing respectively a roll, staccato sounds, and rolls and staccato sounds combined. Three different sizes of maracas are used:

Ex. 97

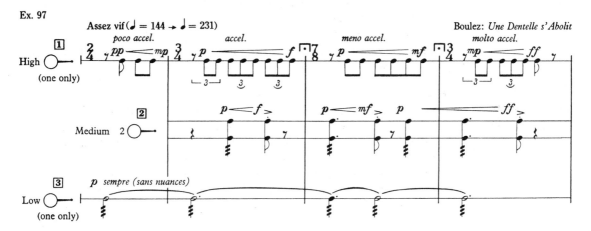

Boulez: *Une Dentelle s'Abolit*

The volume of maracas is small and they are only suitable for use in small ensembles. The dynamic range in the last example (pp to ff) exaggerates their real capabilities.

Cabaca

This instrument, of Brazilian origin, is similar to a maraca but much larger in size. It is made out of a large gourd or coconut, emptied and dried. Like a maraca, it is fitted with a handle, but as well as having dried seeds or shot inside, there is a net of beads fitted outside the gourd.

The cabaca is usually played by rotating the handle in the right hand while the left holds the net of beads and prevents its rotation. There is therefore a double sound effect—the roll of the seeds inside the gourd and the rattle of the beads on the external surface. The cabaca may be shaken like the maracas, in which case the staccato sound is less precise, because the bead net continues to move after the gourd itself has been arrested.

Mexican Bean
This is a dried bean about twelve inches long, actually the fruit of a tropical tree. The dried seeds produce the characteristic rattling sound of the maracas when the bean is shaken, but the sound is sharper and more precise.

Chocolo or Ka-Me-So
This Latin American instrument is sometimes an empty dried gourd of virtually cylindrical shape, about 13 in. (33 cm.) long, sometimes a metal cylinder of about the same length and 4 in. (10 cm.) in diameter with each end sealed off. The inside is partly filled with shot, dried seeds, or rice. It may be held at the centre with one hand, or at each end with both. It may be agitated by a gentle rolling motion of the wrists, or the shot or seeds may be made to run from end to end.

The chocolo gives the same effect as the maraca roll, but the tone is more gentle and the roll more legato. The metal version however, produces a less attractive sound with a pronounced metallic ring.

Guiro or Rape
The guiro, guero, or rape is a dried empty gourd of elongated shape about 13 in. (33 cm.) long, cut with evenly-spaced serrations. In authentic models, one end is thin and the other fairly broad. The left thumb is inserted in a special hole at the thin end, and while the left hand grasps the instrument, a special thin wood scraper is stroked over the serrations with the right hand. This produces a hard, rasping sound. Commercial models are made in hardwood and have a cylindrical shape with a torpedo-like point at each end.

Stravinsky uses the guiro in the 'Cortège du Sage' section of *The Rite of Spring*, where the whole orchestra plays a violent fortissimo ostinato. The guiro plays a simple eight-in-a-bar rhythm with up and down strokes of the scraper. In *Ionisation*, Varèse gives the guiro rapid rhythms:

Ex. 98

Varèse: *Ionisation*

In *Kontakte*, Stockhausen indicates the instrument to be scraped intermittently during stick work on drums, bongos, cowbell etc.

The instrument has a rough, rustic quality of sound which is more suited to robust sonorities than to delicate atmospheres. There is an up-and-down scooping of the pitch, due to differences in the velocity of scraping. This effect hardly lends itself to serious music, but could be used with advantage on more light-hearted occasions.

Reco-reco
This rasped instrument is similar to the guiro, but is made of bamboo with serrations cut in the surface. The bamboo reco-reco (or 'reso-reso') has a more woody sound than the guiro, with a slight hollowness in the tone. The reco-reco is sometimes made from a cow horn.

Villa-Lobos, in his *Uira purú*, indicates that the instrument is to be beaten as well as rasped.

Jaw Bone
This Latin American instrument is made from the jaw bone of an ass. The teeth are removed and then re-fastened in place by short springs or strings, so that they move within their cavities. The jaw bone is held in the left hand and struck with the right, so that the teeth shake with a sharp, staccato sound, making a harsh rattle something like when marbles are struck together. Sometimes small bells are hung on the jaw bone to add a tinkling sound.

The instrument is usually used with an ostinato rhythm in fast music such as the conga.

Rattle or Ratchet
In the cog-rattle, a hard resonant blade of wood is held in a frame in such a position that it is caught by the teeth of a wooden cog when the latter revolves, making a loud clacking sound. In modern orchestral ratchets, the instrument is 'V'-shaped with a wood blade in each leg of the 'V'. The cog is at the apex and is turned with a metal handle. In this way, a more or less continuous sound can be obtained.

A simpler rattle consists of a handle fixed to the cog, round which the frame containing the wooden blade is whirled. An even, continuous sound cannot however, be obtained with this instrument, due to the jerky movement. Nevertheless, it can add a kind of lively 'brio' to the sound.

The most celebrated use of the rattle is in Strauss's *Till Eulenspiegel* at the moment when the hero bursts tempestuously into the market place. It has been used to imitate gunfire (e.g. in Beethoven's *Wellington's Victory*), but mostly its cracking whirr has been exploited to give a colourful breeziness to music of light-hearted nature (e.g. de Falla's *El Retablo de Maese Pedro*,

Siegmeister's *Sunday in Brooklyn*, etc.). Nevertheless, it has been used in more serious scores such as Pizzetti's *Agamenone*, Milhaud's *The Death of a Tyrant*, and even in abstract music (e.g. Varèse's *Hyperprism*).

Cuica, String Drum, or Lion's Roar

The cuica is a lesser-known Latin American instrument, possibly a variant of the Neapolitan putipù. One form is made with a slightly cone-shaped metal or earthenware shell, over the top end of which is stretched a drumskin. A wood stick is fastened in the centre of the skin and usually covered with rosin. When the stick is rubbed with a damp sponge or wash leather, vibrations are transmitted to the drumskin, producing sounds which can hardly be called musical in quality. One authority says the cuica 'suggests the sound of the cuckoo', but it is a cuckoo with a very broken voice. To the author the sound is more like the bark of an African bull-frog suffering from flatulence.

The string drum or 'lion's roar' is very similar, except that a rosined string takes the place of the wooden stick. This is held taut and rubbed in the same way. The shell may be wooden and the head made of parchment. In some cases, the end of the taut string is tied to a round piece of wood. When this is turned, it grips the string and then lets it go, thus setting up vibrations which are transmitted to the membrane. This method of playing permits accurate control of the sounds emitted.

String drums can vary considerably in size. Some are quite small and emit a puny sound, but the true 'lion's roar' is as large as a bucket and can give out a fearsome sound.

Varèse uses the string drum in *Ionisation*, mostly with a quick crescendo, piano to forte, and less often in quiet dynamics with small crescendos and diminuendos. These usages are obviously associated with the two ways of playing the instrument—(a) a quick, forceful rub of the stick or string, and (b) a less energetic up-and-down motion.

The cuica is to be heard in Latin American music of a more earthy type, now and then emitting its vulgar blurt.

A similar effect to the cuica has been obtained by rubbing a rosined glove or cloth over a snare drum stick with the tip of the stick pressed against the centre of the drum head (cf. Russel, Concerto for Eight Percussion Instruments).

Sand Blocks

A few scores indicate the use of sandpaper blocks. These are two blocks of wood with strips of sandpaper tightly stretched over one surface in the manner of a cabinet-maker's sanding tool. The blocks are held one in each hand and rubbed together to give a dry shuffling sound. Alternatively one block may be clamped in a fixed position so that only one hand need be used.

The sound is on a low dynamic scale, and could be used in many situations where a quiet, hissing, background sound is called for. The sand blocks may be rubbed together in free time to give a 'tremolo', or they can produce a rhythmic shuffle in fixed tempo.

Switch
A bundle of dry hard twigs tied together has occasionally been used (Mahler's Seventh Symphony, Varèse's *Integrales*) to strike a drum head, or the skin or shell of a bass drum, producing a harsh, swishing sound. Varèse uses the switch on a bass drum shell together with a wire brush, with precise, forceful rhythms.

The switch could be used to replace the wire brush, either on drums or cymbals, where a more powerful effect is required than can be obtained by wire brushes alone.

Thunder Effects
There is a 'thunder sheet' made from a large piece of thin tin or metal alloy, which when shaken produces a sound like thunder-cracks due to the buckling and crumpling of the sheet. It used to be part of stage properties, but is now largely superseded by recordings played on amplifying equipment.

A 'thunder machine' is used in Strauss's *Alpine Symphony*, made by placing heavy balls inside a large drum and rotating this on a pivot.

However, thunder effects are now rather *passé*, especially since electronic music has carried this type of sound into realms which go far beyond the purely naturalistic field.

Wind Machine
The wind machine is made of a large cylindrical wood framework covered with silk, revolved by turning a handle. The silk is stroked by fixed pieces of cardboard or thin wood so that as the barrel is turned a swirling sound is produced which turns into a whistle as the revolving of the barrel is accelerated. This instrument is usually employed only for realistic effects (cf. Strauss's *Don Quixote* and *Alpine Symphony*), and it has been quite superseded by electronic sounds (principally 'white sound') which are available on gramophone records for theatrical use.

DRUMMING TECHNIQUES. ROLLS. ENDING ROLLS. SHORT ROLLS
THE FLAM. THE DRAG AND RUFF. THE PARADIDDLE AND
REVERSED PARADIDDLE. THE RIM SHOT. MUFFLING
DRUM STICKS AND BEATERS. FINGER-STYLE PLAYING
TONAL CONTRASTS. PITCH DISTORTION

THE SNARE OR SIDE DRUM. THE TENOR DRUM. TOMTOMS. BONGOS
CONGAS. TIMBALES. COCKTAIL DRUM. BASS DRUM
TAMBOURINE. PROVENÇAL TAMBOURINE. AFRICAN DRUM
CHINESE DRUM

Drumming Techniques

It is certainly possible to write fairly well for drums without considering
drumming techniques in the least. But there is no doubt that better results
will be more consistently obtained after a little study of the standard drum
'rudiments'.

There are two reasons for this. Firstly, drummers acquire their skill in a
special way. In most cases, they learn the snare drum techniques first of all,
and then apply these to any other drums they may have to play. Therefore,
if our drum parts are based on a knowledge of the rudiments, they will be
interpreted skilfully and with zest. If they are not based on the rudiments,
the results may not come up to our expectations. The second reason is simply
that the rudiments can be so highly effective. Not only are they effective, they
are the essence of drum language. Flams, drags, ruffs, and rolls are not merely
decorations, they are the instrument's way of speaking. Any drum scoring
which ignores such rudiments runs the risk of being inarticulate, of stammer-
ing haltingly rather than speaking out with crisp vigour and fluency.

Though knowledge of the rudiments is so important, a detailed description
of them is outside the scope of this book. The following notes are merely a
summary of the most vital points which concern composers and arrangers.
The techniques discussed will be mainly those for the snare drum, as these
are the basis of most drum playing.

Rolls

Rolls are produced by rapid successions of drum strokes, producing an even, sustained sound. There are two types of roll, one played with separate beats (the 'single stroke roll' used for timpani), the other with rebounding strokes (the 'daddy-mammy roll' used for the snare drum). Drum rolls are usually indicated by the tremolo sign ( ) but with timpani the sign 'tr.⁓' is customary. If rolls extend over bar lines, the notes should be tied, otherwise it is not clear whether accentuation is intended at the beginning of each bar.

Rolls need not be smooth, but can be interspersed with accents which, especially at a fast tempo, can be vividly exciting:

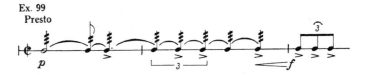

Ex. 99
Presto

Rolls can be graduated in volume with ease and good effect, while tone variations are possible by rolling at different beating spots. Very quiet purring rolls can be played near the rim, while near the centre the tone is virile and rough.

Ending rolls

It is important to show precisely how rolls should end. The following example shows various possibilities:

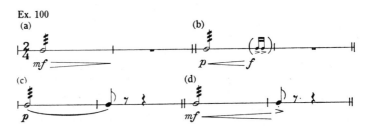

Ex. 100
(a)   (b)

(c)   (d)

In example (a) the roll dies away without any beat in bar two, while in (b) there is a crescendo which again does not end with a note in the second bar. However, a couple of strong alternate strokes can end the crescendo, as shown in parentheses.

A more frequent occurrence is to end *on* a beat as in (c) and (d). In (c) the the roll is held piano throughout, and is unbroken before ending without an accent on the first quaver in bar 2. In (d) the roll has a crescendo and ends with a definite accent in bar 2.

Short rolls
These can add verve and brilliance to drum parts, particularly as preparations
for accented beats, though they are also effective *on* beats. As drummers will
choose one of the many roll rudiments for the performance of any short roll,
it is essential to indicate the exact tempo of the music, the exact duration of
the roll, and the position of any special accents. For instance, the following
example indicates that rolls should be quavers ending with accents on the
beats, but according to the tempo the drummer will choose a rudiment which
may comprise from five to fifteen strokes or more:

Ex. 101

The Flam
This is a grace note played lightly immediately before a heavier downstroke.
It is used as an *ornament* to enrich rhythmic designs as at (a) below, or to give
accentuation to downstrokes as at (b):

Ex. 102   Walton: *Belshazzar's Feast*

Flams serve also to broaden and give more substance to isolated notes or
unaccentuated short notes, which would otherwise sound rather meagre and
ineffective.

Drags and Ruffs
These valuable rudiments comprise two and three strokes respectively before
a main downstroke (drag: ♫ ♩, ruff: ♫♫ ♩). It is important to indicate
whether 'closed' or 'open' drags and ruffs are required.
    Closed drags and ruffs have two or three light rebounding strokes (played
by the same hand) crushed in immediately before a downstroke. They give
accentuation to a downstroke, or merely *broaden* its sound in a smooth manner.
They must always be indicated with slurs thus: ♫ ♩ and ♫♫ ♩.

Open drags and ruffs are played with separate strokes for each note. The effect is more defined and deliberate, and is suitable only for *embellishments*. Do not use slurs.

Drags and ruffs could be used much more in concert music than has been the case. They are absolutely essential if drum parts are to sound fluent and significant.

The Paradiddle and Reversed Paradiddle

These rudiments are essential features of drumming technique, but their exact nature need not be elaborated here. Their principal use is to give a smoother, more legato effect to rapidly repeated strokes than is possible if the notes are played with 'single sticking'. Hand-to-hand strokes produce a staccato effect, and if this is required it should be indicated. In the paradiddle and reversed paradiddle, rebounding strokes are introduced which smooth out the note successions considerably. At the same time, a great variety of accentuation can be introduced, and also embellishments such as the closed drag. If smooth note repetitions are required, a general legato indication should be given, and any accentuations and embellishments indicated. The performer will then use the rebounding strokes of these rudiments as he thinks most appropriate.

The Rim-shot

This produces a loud crack, said to resemble the report of a revolver. Rim shots are most effective where a very loud accent is required. They may be played in two ways, as 'stick rim-shots' or as 'hoop-cracks'.

For *stick rim-shots* the tip of the left stick is placed on the centre of the vellum, while the shaft of the stick is laid over the rim. The left stick is then struck hard with the right. Naturally this rim-shot needs a moment of preparation.

The *hoop crack* instead can be played at any moment by striking both the rim and the vellum simultaneously with the same stick. The sound is not as forceful as the stick rim-shot. For this reason, and also because of the ease with which hoop-cracks can be made, this form of rim-shot is most suitable for mixing with normal drum strokes.

Rim-shots can be indicated as follows:

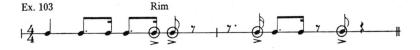

Ex. 103   Rim

Muffling

All drums may be muffled or muted by covering the batter head with a cloth.

This deadens and darkens the sound considerably. This effect is sometimes indicated by the Italian *coperto*. The muffling of snare drums is excellent, as it produces a light, thin tone. Performers often partially muffle their instruments by placing a small square of felt on the vellum. This removes excessive ring from the drums.

Drum Sticks and Beaters

Though wooden snare drum sticks are most commonly used for drum playing, xylophone and other tuned percussion beaters are also frequently used.

It is natural that a percussionist whose main task is snare drum work will use the conventional snare drum sticks (unless others are indicated) for all drumming, whether on snare drums or not. On the other hand, players of tuned percussion find it convenient to use xylophone, vibraphone, or marimba beaters when they have to change over to drums, particularly if this has to be done quickly. In any case, they may like to use tuned percussion beaters because they prefer the 'feel' of these to the differently balanced snare drum sticks. However, for the composer, the choice of suitable sticks or beaters should depend on the tonal effects required, not on the conveniences and preferences of the players, though these factors should naturally be borne in mind.

The type of stick or beater used can influence drum sounds in three ways—tone, attack, and volume.

Tone. Whether drums are tuned or not, their sound-spectrum comprises a wide range of different sounds, some low, some high. A thin, hard-headed stick will bring out the higher sounds, the drum sounding 'bright' and clear. A soft-headed, broad stick will elicit the low tones: the sound will be mellow, dark, even muffled, if the beater is very soft. Soft beaters are best for eliciting sounds of definite pitch.

Attack. The kind of attack emitted by a drum depends on the resilience of the stick or beater head. Hard beaters will produce a crisp, well-defined attack. Soft beaters will give a less distinct delivery, the edges of the sounds will be rounded. In short, the attack will be 'smothered' by the spread of the beater head at each new contact with the drumskin.

Volume. The spread of soft beater heads produces a damping effect, and the volume of sound is reduced accordingly. On the other hand, hard beaters, being virtually inflexible, will produce maximum vibration of the vellum, with no damping effect. Hard beaters are therefore most suited to loud dynamics, soft beaters to quiet passages.

However, it must be stressed that percussion players are trained to produce the widest ranges of volume with snare drum sticks, so these can be used even for pianissimo, if a bright sound is needed, with crisp attack.

Types of Sticks and Beaters. Depending, therefore, on the kind of tone, attack, and volume required, the following sticks and beaters may be used:

Hard
Snare drum sticks. Xylophone or vibraphone beaters with round heads, in wood, plastic, or hard rubber.

Medium hard
Xylophone or vibraphone beaters with medium-hard rubber or woven yarn heads.
Timpani sticks with medium felt heads.

Soft
Vibraphone or marimba beaters with soft woven yarn or rubber heads.
Soft timpani sticks.

In the choice of sticks and beaters, there is one very important consideration to be borne in mind. Because of their balance and small, hard heads, only snare drum sticks are really suitable for drumming techniques which require the rebounding type of stroke. When sticks with softer heads are used, rebounding strokes lose their clarity. This means that when tuned percussion beaters or timpani sticks are used for drum playing, rebounding strokes should be avoided. Normally, with these kinds of sticks and beaters, drum rudiments are played hand-to-hand with alternate strokes of each stick, the player only using double beats as an occasional convenience.

The use of brushes. Wire brushes produce a swishing, rustling sound when the brush is swept or dragged across the drum head. Alternatively, they can be used instead of sticks to play the normal drum rudiments (though rebounding strokes are not possible). In this case the brushes produce a brisk, flapping kind of sound which can give excellent rhythmic results.

Furthermore, it is possible to produce these two rhythmic effects simultaneously. While one hand plays a swishing drag across the vellum, the other can play single-stroke rhythms either on the same drum head, or on the cymbals or other drums, so that quite complex rhythmic effects are possible.

The volume scale is much reduced when brushes are used. Brush strokes can be indicated as follows:

$$\mathsf{X} = \text{single strokes.}$$

$$\mathsf{X} \wedge \wedge \wedge = \text{brush dragged across the drum head.}$$

Finger-style Playing

All drums can be played with either the fingers or the flat of the hands, or both. As drum sounds are most resonant, and the attack is crispest, when the vellum is allowed to vibrate freely, in finger playing an elastic, bouncing stroke should be used, the fingers leaving the drum-head as soon as possible after it is struck. A 'glancing-off' stroke is most effective, and produces the best tone.

The patterns of strokes used can be quite complex. Rolls can be executed in many ways (with two fingers of one hand, with both hands, with a rolling movement of the thumb and little finger, etc.) and all the usual flams, drags, ruffs, and paradiddles performed with ease. Indeed, even more complex rhythms can be played with finger techniques than with drum sticks. For each hand can play different rhythmic patterns at the same time.

For instance, the following separate patterns for each hand can be played, using either a single drum, or two or more different-sized instruments:

Ex. 104

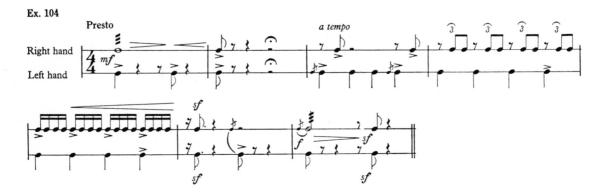

Right hand

Left hand

In addition, different tones can be obtained by striking drums at or near the centre, or near the rim (see also next section). In general, the tone of sounds played near the centre is deeper than that produced near the rim. These tonal contrasts can be of excellent effect, particularly when a number of different sized drums are used, so that a wide gamut of pitches is available.

In his *Amores*, John Cage writes for nine tomtoms, played by three percussionists, each having three instruments graduated in pitch and size. Each drum is played at the centre and near the rim. In the notation, notes between the lines indicate playing near or at the centres of the three drum-heads, whereas notes on lines indicate playing near the rims. Each player has therefore six different tones, indicated in ascending order of pitch, thus:

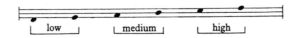

The following is an example from this charming piece:

Ex. 105   John Cage: *Amores*

etc.

Finger style playing can produce still more tonal effects than Cage uses in *Amores*. The fingers can produce high notes on the rim, a fingernail flicked on the vellum will produce a sharp crack, the drum may be struck a glancing, rotating blow so that successive fingers of the hand hit the skin, producing a compressed roll of sforzando character, the fingers of one hand can be used to muffle the drum, or can press the vellum to raise its pitch and so on. Drums can also be played by friction. The thumb or finger can be pushed hard across the vellum to produce either a brief 'lion's roar', or a mere prolonged rumbling.

In finger-style playing, contact with the vellum can be made by either the soft fleshy finger tips, the knuckles, or the ends of the fingernails. This gives a notable tonal contrast. However, such small subtleties of playing (and there are many others) are not easy to indicate in scores, and it is perhaps best to leave players some liberty to use their own invention. Any attempt to indicate a variety of strokes in finger playing is bound to produce a confused, illegible notation, which will inhibit the player rather than encourage him to give his best.

Playing with the flat of the hand also produces special effects, which are most impressive with big drums, especially timpani. If the hand remains on the vellum after a stroke, a dead, slapping sound results. If the flat hand is withdrawn off the vellum gradually during a number of strokes, a distinct rise in the pitch of sounds is produced (and *vice versa*). Naturally such strokes are only possible on rimless drums.

Finger-style playing is at a considerably lower dynamic scale than that of normal drum techniques. Though this makes the style suitable for quiet orchestral passages only, it is ideal for playing in chamber ensembles. In fact, there is no reason why drums should not be used in chamber music of the most delicate nature, now that finger playing can produce such quiet sounds.

Tonal contrasts

With all drums, especially those with single heads, there is a distinct difference in tone and apparent pitch between notes played near the centre and those near the rim. Notes played near the rim give an impression of high pitch. As one moves across the vellum towards the centre, the sounds deepen. This change in pitch is due to the changing prominence of the fundamental tone and its harmonics. Consequently the timbre changes from 'bright' near the rim to 'dark' at the centre. In fact, at the exact centre, some drums give a very dead sound. This change of timbre occurs whether drums are tuned or not. Snare drums are a special case. While the sound from the snared head is the same high-pitched sound wherever the batter head is struck, the latter changes its tones just as other drums do.

Open-ended drums with single heads (bongos, congas, timbales, and tom-toms with single heads) produce more evident changes of tone and pitch than double-headed drums.

No notation is standard for indicating drum strokes at the centre of the head, near the rim, etc., so composers usually write 'at the centre' or 'at the rim'. However, in music where rapid changes of beating spot are required, some special notation is essential, and it is suggested that strokes at the centre should be indicated by ringed notes ( ) and those near the rim by triangular-shaped 'white' notes ( ). When neither of these signs are used, the player should return to the normal beating spot.

Pitch distortion in slack drum heads

When drums or timpani are tuned to low sounds, the heads will be slack and a certain amount of pitch distortion will occur. Under a heavy blow, a drum with a slack head will emit a sound of deeper pitch than that to which it has been tuned, and after the impact the pitch will rise as the head returns to its normal shape. This causes a scooping, glissando effect, which may or may not be objectionable. Such effects are not normally desired, but can be very suitable where less refined atmospheres are called for. They can sound virile, even savage. In the *Rite of Spring*, the cannon shots of the bass drum can sound much more riotous and fierce if there is a pronounced scoop. Big African drums similarly have a fascinating, rude sound precisely because of their characteristic pitch distortions. If tomtoms are tuned as low as possible, with a minimum of tension on the heads, they can produce a much less refined sound than usual.

With slack heads, it is possible to obtain glissandos and pitch alterations by pressing hard on the vellum, preferably with the left elbow. Jazz drummers use this effect, but it does not seem to occur in concert scores.

The Snare or Side Drum

The orchestral snare drum is a double-headed instrument about 14 in. (35 cm.) in diameter and between 5 and 8 in. (13 and 20 cm.) deep. Snares (strands of gut or wire) are stretched across the lower or 'snare' head. When the batter head is struck, the lower vellum vibrates against the snares (which in turn rebound) producing an even rattling sound of high pitch. The snares can be quickly lowered away from the snare head by a special mechanism, so that the drum produces a deeper sound similar to a tomtom of equivalent size.

Thin snare drums only 3 in. (8 cm.) deep can be used as a tonal contrast to normal-sized drums. Their crisp, high-pitched tone is particularly suited to light passages. This so-called 'pancake' drum is particularly favoured in France, where it is termed the 'tarole'.

The snare drum is usually played with wooden sticks about 16 in. (40 cm.) long, which have tapered ends and a small olive-shaped knob at the extremity. These sticks particularly favour the use of the rebounding strokes already discussed in the 'rudiments'. Occasionally soft-headed sticks are used, with the snares 'off', to obtain a soft, mellow sound. In this case rebounding strokes lose their clarity, so single-sticking is preferable.

In writing for the snare drum, it is well to bear the following points in mind:

(1) If the drum part is too simple (e.g. sparse, detached notes) it will probably sound lame and feeble. The snare drum is usually employed for its ability to give an ebullient energy to the music. This it is only able to do through note patternings of a relatively 'exuberant' nature—hence the traditional embellishments such as the flam, drag, ruff, and short roll. The spirit of the instrument lies in elaboration through the use of such figures, so we must not hesitate to use them where they are appropriate:

Ex. 106   Mahler: *Symphony No. 3*

Schwungvoll

(2) The snare drum may be used not only in forte passages. It is capable of contributing delicate effects even at pianissimo.

(3) Rolls should always be functional. Though they can serve as background colour at one dynamic level, the novelty of effect soon wears off. Crescendo rolls are often used to support an orchestral crescendo. The opposite effect —a sudden decrescendo—is less frequently used, but is very effective. Fluctuations of dynamics within a long roll, coupled with accentuations, can be striking, if they have purpose.

(4) The snare drum is not suited to performing long drawn-out crescendos and diminuendos. These should be brief, a few bars at the most.

(5) Notation should be as precise as possible. For example, performers should be left in no doubt as to how a roll finishes, or how a given passage should be accentuated. Snare drum sounds are very brief, so that long notes (minims and semibreves) will seldom be used for single sounds. However, there is little point in writing the part in very short duration values (semiquavers or quavers) if the number of rests used is going to create a visually confusing pattern. Clarity should be the ideal.

The sound of the snare drum is dry and energetic, even belligerent. For many of us it inevitably has military associations, and perhaps for this reason it shows a tendency to fall out of use in contemporary music, especially now that so many other membrane instruments are available.

The Tenor Drum
This drum is similar in diameter to the snare drum, but is considerably deeper, between 10 and 12 in. (26 and 30 cm.). Continental tenor drums of the 'cassa rullante' type may be deeper still, with shells up to 20 in. (50 cm.) long. In all other respects this drum is similar to the snare drum, except that normally the orchestral tenor drum has no snares.

It is usually played with felt-headed beaters, but for a harder tone snare drum sticks can be used. Its tone is sombre and dark, with a certain dull, thudding quality, which seems to give the sound a lugubrious medieval character. This is particularly so when the drum is used in the traditional way as a 'rolling' drum.

In the orchestra, the tenor drum has been used for its suggestion of menace, or simply as a drum pitched between the snare drum and bass drum.

However, now that tomtoms are commonly employed for such variations in pitch, the tenor drum is less often used. Nevertheless, it is still valuable for its distinctive tone quality. No other drum can give such a suggestion of ill omen, or so fittingly accompany a 'march to the scaffold'.

Britten makes use of these associations of the tenor drum with fate and death in the *Libera Me* section of his *War Requiem*. The tenor and bass drums begin the movement solo with a stern, inexorable march rhythm which dominates the whole movement:

Ex. 107   Britten: *War Requiem*

Tomtoms

Tomtoms are unsnared drums made with laminated wood shells, and have double heads which can be separately tensioned. Occasional models are made with single heads.

As tomtoms are used for drum sounds of a wide variety of pitch, but with similar timbre throughout the range, they are usually sold in a number of different sizes: some firms make at least seven. The diameter of tomtoms can be between 12 and 18 in. (30 and 45 cm.), the depth between 8 and 20 in. (20 and 50 cm.).

The larger tomtoms are supported on legs. The smaller ones can be clamped together in pairs on a special support. In any case they must be grouped close together for convenience of playing. The largest drum is usually on the left and the others arranged in decreasing order of size from left to right. However, other drum layouts can often be ideal (e.g. three drums in a triangle, or four in a square), especially if the music is written with such arrangements in mind.

The tone of tomtoms is relatively pure, without the barbaric suggestion their name implies. They have no distinctive characteristics like the menacing tenor drum, the rattling bongos and timbales, and the combative snare drum. Like the timpani, their sound is pure enough for them to be inserted easily into orchestral music, simply as 'musical' sounds. Nevertheless, their timbre and attack can be influenced by the choice of stick or beater. Snare drum sticks will as usual give a bright, ringing tone with a hard attack. Soft sticks will take the edge off the attack and mellow the timbre. They produce less overtones and the drums are more defined in pitch, and can sound almost like timpani.

Tomtoms are most frequently used as instruments of indefinite pitch, the composer usually requesting merely 'low', 'medium', or 'high' sounds. Sometimes, indeed, composers do not specify tomtoms, but merely 'drums' of various pitch. In this case tomtoms will be used, as they are the only large group of drums of varied pitch which have a unified tone colour and are easily available.

If tomtoms are used as instruments of indefinite pitch (as is normal), the player will tune the two drum heads of each instrument differently. In addition, he will probably use a 'tone control' usually incorporated in tomtoms, by which small internal dampers are pressed against the batter head. These eliminate the fundamental tone, leaving only overtones sounding. Playing near the rim also enhances overtones.

Tomtoms can be accurately tuned. Single-headed instruments have the deepest and purest sounds (they can be quite mellow with soft beaters) and can be tuned roughly within the timpani range. Double-headed drums are higher-pitched and can be tuned up to a tone or so above middle C. However, when drumskins are tensioned excessively, their tone deteriorates and the drum sounds 'knocky'. On the other hand, heads can be slackened quite a lot before the tone deteriorates. It is therefore best to avoid high tunings and use the following compass:

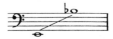

Even though tomtoms have fundamental tones in such a deep range, they seem to sound much higher, especially when hard sticks are used.

As the instruments available are likely to be of different sizes (e.g. large, medium, and small), it is best to decide on tunings in well-separated pitch zones. In any case, in order to distinguish easily between the sounds of different tomtoms, they must be tuned at least a major third apart, preferably more. Untuned instruments should similarly be of contrasting pitch.

Tomtoms can be used as substitutes for high timpani, or to carry timpani sounds into a higher pitch zone. For instance, in the *Prelude* of *Agon*, Stravinsky uses three tomtoms in a higher register than the three timpani used in the same movement. His desire seems to be for tonal unity, rather than colour contrast between timpani and tomtoms:

Ex. 108   Stravinsky: *Agon*

The following passage illustrates a few effects which are characteristic of music for tomtoms:

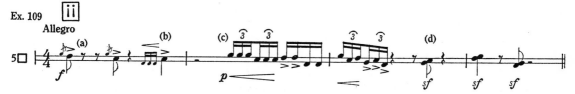

In (a) are shown flams using different drums for each stroke, while in (b) the last note in the first bar is embellished by an open ruff played on the lowest drum and passing on to the middle drum for the final accentuated note. Such ruffs and drags 'over the drums' are particularly effective.

In (c) is shown some typical passage work using all five tomtoms, first with repeated notes and then with a rapid cascade of single strokes on each drum to end the phrase. Such fast passage work has a brilliance which can hardly be equalled by any other membrane instruments. The example ends in (d) with sforzando strokes on two drums at once—a powerful effect.

Rolls 'over the drums' are possible, and if well played can be fascinating. Unfortunately players tend to break off the rolls when passing from one drum to another. For this reason, dotted slurs can be written to indicate that the rolls should be unbroken:

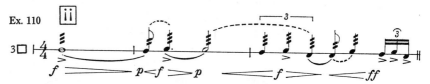

Note the dynamic changes. These make such rolls much more telling than when the volume is unchanging.

In writing rolls 'over the drums', it is important to bear in mind the distance between drums. Where drums are close together, it is comparatively easy to change from drum to drum without breaking the roll. But if they are far apart (e.g. the 'outside' drums of a group of five) this will be very difficult to achieve smoothly. However, if drums are grouped in a close circle, these problems disappear.

It is possible to include flams, drags, or ruffs within a rolling passage, with 'decorating' notes on different drums from the rolls. Continuity in the rolls is again indicated in the following example by dotted slurs, but these are omitted in the middle of the second bar, to indicate that the ruff to the note on the third beat should be attacked clearly:

Finger-style playing
Tomtoms are particularly suited to the finger-style playing which has already been fully discussed on pages 114–115. There is little to add here, except to stress that the volume scale is small and the general effect gentle and unforced—characteristics which make this style suitable for use in chamber music ensembles.

Single-headed tomtoms
Tomtoms are usually sold with double heads, but some players remove the lower head in order to get a drum sound which they regard as preferable. With a single head, the drum has a deeper, mellow sound, which is 'open', without so much of the normal tomtom's muffled, indeterminate 'boom'. The tone is clear, round, and tuneful when the head is not too tight (especially with soft beaters) and is admirable where pitch precision is desirable. If, however, indeterminate sounds are preferred, the vellum can be damped (with a tone control or by a piece of felt laid on the head) and the drum will be bright and forceful, especially so with a tight head, which gives a cracking 'surface' tone.

Ludwig make a set of four single-headed tomtoms specially suited to tuning in the higher pitch range (up to G above middle C). Their diameters range from 6 to 12 in. (15 to 30 cm.). These instruments could be coupled with larger tomtoms where a very wide pitch range is required (e.g. in *Gruppen*, Stockhausen requires 12 tomtoms 'and/or tumbas and bongos' which cover the enormous pitch range from two octaves below middle C to the G above).

Wooden-headed tomtoms
See 'wood-plate drums' under 'wood drums' in the previous chapter.

Bongos
These small Latin-American instruments, probably of primitive origin, are still made in a very simple way. In Cuba, short sections of tree trunks are hollowed out, producing shells of somewhat conic shape and quite thick section. Drum skins are stretched over the larger ends and nailed into position.

Before use, the skins are held near a source of heat so that they become very taut. The drums are usually played in pairs, one larger than the other.

Factory-made bongos retain most of the characteristics of the original drums, though in some cases the shells are coopered. They are usually made in pairs, or occasionally in groups of three, and are fastened together so that they may be held between the knees for playing in the authentic manner. They still have slightly cone-shaped thick wooden shells, and the drums are without high rims, so that they may be played by the hands or fingers without inconvenience.

Each bongo is about 5 in. (13 cm.) deep. The smaller instrument has a diameter of about 6 in. (15 cm.) while the larger one is usually about 8 in. (20 cm.) across. They have single heads, fitted with tension screws for tuning. Bongo heads are highly tensioned, so as to give their characteristic sharp, snappy tone.

When bongos are played in Latin-American music, they are held between the knees (the player being seated) with the larger drum on the right. In orchestral playing (or in jazz groups) the bongos are fitted on a special stand, and players prefer the largest drum on the left, as with tomtoms.

The bongos can be played with the fingers or the flat of the hand, near the centres or near the rims, in a great variety of tones and pitches. The tone is rather dry and snappy with strokes near the rims, more hollow and deeper-toned at the centres. Such tonal contrasts are a prominent characteristic of bongo music and players are usually expert at producing them.

Pitch contrasts are also much favoured, and the players tune their instruments so as to cover a wide pitch range. Bongos can give sounds of a fairly definite pitch, so that a 'tuned' group of timpani, tomtoms, and bongos is theoretically possible. But in practice bongo sounds are so easily distorted that it is best to disregard the possibility of accurate tuning.

Played finger-style, their volume is restricted. With forcible playing, the sounds crack and tonal shadings go by the board. Instead, small wooden sticks (such as timbale sticks about 8 in. (20 cm.) long) can be used for louder volumes. These give crisp, cracking sounds of high pitch, and energetic character. Soft felt or yarn heads can be used to simulate finger style playing, but the result will hardly equal the subtle shadings that fingers can produce.

In Latin-American music bongos are among the few instruments which do not play repeated ostinatos of conventional pattern. Players may extemporize freely, and usually show off with complex rhythms and rapid patterings. In fact the genius of the instruments lies in brilliant flourishes and a kind of chattering, insistent commentary. The following example is a synthesis of typical bongo rhythms. Unfortunately contrasts of tone and pitch cannot be indicated adequately in notation; they are here omitted:

Ex. 112

Bongos can be combined with larger single-headed drums of similar type, such as congas, to exploit a wider pitch range. As congas are also made in pairs, and can also produce a wide variety of sounds, the combined resources of these two instruments are worth exploitation. They can be used in chamber ensembles with finger-style playing, even when the music is of an abstract character, as in Toshiro Mayuzumi's *Microcosmos*:

Ex. 113

Toshiro Mayuzumi: *Microcosmos*

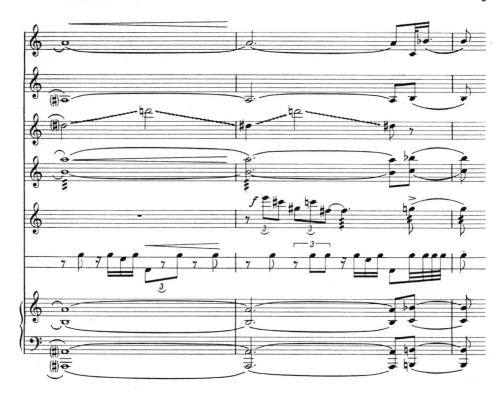

Very smooth, subdued rolls can be obtained by turning a bongo upside down and placing a handful of dried peas on the vellum. The peas can be swirled round evenly, or shaken to produce occasional accents.

Congas

Conga drums or 'tumbas' are similar in origin to bongos, and much of the information already given for the latter is equally valid for congas. They are single-headed drums of about 10 to 12 in. (26 to 30 cm.) diameter, with a long, tapering, thick wooden shell between 25 and 29 in. (64 and 74 cm.) long. Sometimes the shell has a bulbous shape, and may be coopered. Like bongos, congas have depressed rims, leaving the head free for finger-style playing.

In Latin-American music sometimes only one conga is used. In this case the instrument is held between the knees or carried across the chest by means of a sling. When congas are played in pairs, they are supported on an adjustable stand, so that the player can be seated, or stand with the instruments at a suitable height.

Pairs of congas are always tuned to noticeably different pitches, even though the instruments may be exactly the same size, by screw tension rods fixed on the depressed rim. Conga membranes are usually very thick and highly tensioned.

They are usually played with the fingers or flat of the hands, and as with the bongos, a wide variety of tone and pitch can be obtained by striking the heads near the centres or the rims.

The tone is deep and resonant with strokes at the centre of the head, brighter and higher in pitch near the rim. With wooden drum sticks, a more incisive tone is produced.

Though congas may be used with bongos, it must be borne in mind that as congas speak in a relatively low register and with less crispness, the parts written for them should not be as agile as those written for bongos. However, as with bongos, the conga 'language' usually consists of a persistent chatter. Stockhausen uses this as a background ostinato in the entire first section of his *Kreuzspiel*:

Ex. 114   Stockhausen: *Kreuzspiel*

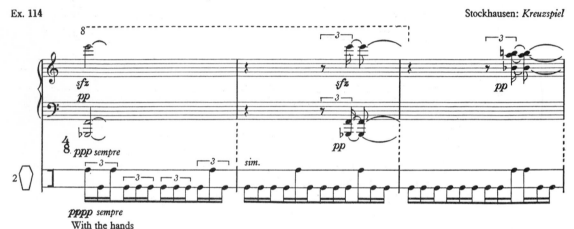

With the hands

Timbales

Like bongos and congas, timbales are of Latin-American origin, and are single-headed instruments usually played in pairs. However, as they are normally intended to be played with wooden sticks (to give a bright, ringing tone) the rims project above the head and the shells are shallow and made of brass or copper. The membranes should be highly tensioned.

Pairs of timbales are usually made in different sizes, having cylindrical shells of different diameter, but the same depth. They are usually 7 to 9 in. (18 to 23 cm.) deep and between 9 and 14 in. (23 and 36 cm.) across. The wooden sticks used for timbales are thin and light, only about 8 to 10 in. (20 to 26 cm.) long. The two drums are supported on an adjustable stand, the largest and deepest-sounding on the left. Some manufacturers make timbales in groups of three.

The tone of timbales is metallic and clanging, with a pronounced ring. They give an exciting sound, which is penetrating and virile, yet not in the least monotonous. For timbales can produce a very varied gamut of tones. In fact their popularity is due precisely to this variety in pitch and colour, produced by striking the heads at various points, and playing on the rims and shells.

They do not as yet seem to have been used in orchestral music, though there is little doubt that they could make a vital contribution where blazing sonorities are required. In chamber music and percussion ensembles, timbales are sometimes used to fill the gap between the high-toned bongos and deeper congas—thus making up a group of six single-headed drums. However, timbales do not match bongos and congas in tone when played forcibly with sticks as their clanging sound is very prominent.

In France, as the word 'timbales' means timpani, these drums are known as 'creoles' or 'timbales creoles'.

Cocktail Drum

This is an all-purpose drum for the travelling jazz musician. It is about 16 in. (40 cm.) across and 24 in. (60 cm.) deep, with two heads under separate tension. The drum is raised up on legs, and has a foot pedal which can be used to strike the lower skin (the cocktail drum is usually played standing). The upper head has a snare fitted underneath so that it can be played as a snare drum. By releasing the snare, a deep tomtom tone can be produced.

This drum therefore serves as snare drum, tomtom, and bass drum. A cymbal and cow bell attached to the rim complete the percussion set. Such an outfit is ideal for the travelling musician or entertainer, and for playing in small rooms. It is also useful where an outfit has to be quickly carried on to a stage and off again.

Bass Drum

There are two main types of orchestral bass drum, one with a single head, the other with two heads. The latter is often favoured, but it should be fairly large, about 36 in. (90 cm.) in diameter. The two skins should be tuned to slightly different intonations, so that a deep sound of apparently indefinite pitch is produced. In this way bass drum sounds fuse well with the orchestral bass, the one complementing the other. The drum is made to seem in tune, while the orchestral bass is given added depth and resonance.

The single-headed drum does not fuse so well with the orchestra, especially if it is too small. However, these so-called 'gong drums' can give out a beautifully mellow sound, especially the large ones of about four feet diameter, and they are to be preferred if their more defined pitch can be tolerated.

Bass drums are usually played in a vertical position, but a horizontal position is preferable when the drum has to be played with both hands, or if the player has also to play other drums grouped nearby. Vertical bass drums can be played by a foot pedal. Usually the instrument is played with a heavy beater or timpani sticks, though snare drum sticks can be very effective.

The sounds have length, so their duration should be accurately indicated. Finger damping is used for short notes. Tremolos can be executed with two sticks, or with a double-headed beater using one hand only. The drum may be muffled with a cloth when soft effects are required. Some composers have indicated the use of a switch for a rough, slappy sound.

The bass drum is mainly used for three purposes: to underline orchestral dynamics, for rhythmic figurations, and for colouristic effects.

In a dynamic role, there is no need to illustrate the drum's functions in emphasizing the strong beats of march-type music, or in reinforcing the hammering chords of such a work as Stravinsky's *Rite of Spring*. Such usages are fairly obvious. The only comment to make is that bass drum parts will be most effective if they are simple and direct.

In the following example from Dallapiccola's *Variations for Orchestra*, the bass drum underlines the dynamics of the brass and lower strings, with stresses which are mostly *off* the beat. At the same time the roll gives a grand-iose shuddering depth to the harmony. It is worth noting that though the composer could have used timpani at this point, he preferred the bass drum for its ability to give a low throb to these grave chords:

Ex. 115

Dallapiccola: *Variations for Orchestra*

Sometimes, for dynamic functions, a choice must be made between bass drum and timpani. It must be decided whether a drum of definite or indefinite pitch is preferable. For instance, in the following example from Britten's *War Requiem*, though the drum part could have been played throughout with a pair of pedal timps, the composer preferred the bass drum for its ability to add weight and body to the orchestral bass. In the same movement, where tuned sounds are preferable the timpani are used:

Ex. 116   Britten: *War Requiem*

The following is an example of the use of the bass drum for rhythmic figurations. Though the music is pianissimo, wooden snare drum sticks are used for crisper execution and drier tone. A lighter tone could be obtained if the drum were played near the rim.

Ex. 117   Britten: *War Requiem*

The tremolo or roll can be used to underline a climax, but is very valuable at low volumes to give a solemn colour to the music. Sometimes this colouring effect can also be used with the function of knitting together instrumental passages which would otherwise be a little bare or isolated:

Ex. 118

Dallapiccola: *Variations for Orchestra*

Here, the entry of the soft drum roll is deliberately kept from being prominent, yet as it progresses, it knits together the movement from brass to strings and then to woodwind, giving these mysterious chords a gentle pulsation. Note how the colouring of the chords is passed from the bass drum to the tamtam and back again.

The bass drum has the most potent sound of the whole orchestra. Occasionally it may be given solo fortissimo strokes which sound like cannon shots (cf. Stravinsky's *Rite of Spring*). In fact the drum has been used to simulate artillery in such works as Berlioz's *Damnation of Faust* and Verdi's *Otello*. Its use for thunder effects needs no mention!

In the past, would-be orchestrators have been told that bass drum parts should be very limited (Forsyth recommends playing in 'one to four bars per movement'). This seems a gross exaggeration. The truth is that the bass drum is either suitable for use in a work, or it is not. If it is not, there will be no part. If it is, there is no need to deny it adventurous employment. For instance, the bass drum is featured (often prominently) in most of Britten's *War Requiem*, in movements of very different mood and character. Sometimes it is in use over quite long periods. Yet nobody has complained that the drum has been over-used in this work.

Consideration should be given to the use of two or three different sizes of drum in order to obtain pitch and colour contrasts. This is already a feature of American Drum and Bugle Corps bands, where weight as well as contrast are required.

Finally, the bass drum can be used as a deep timpano for sounds which are below the timpani range. For tuned sounds the gong drum is preferable in this situation.

The Bass Drum in Jazz Sets

A bass drum as used in jazz sets may be useful for multiple percussion work in concert music. It can be set up with attachments for cymbals, cow bells, wood blocks, and tomtoms, and as the drum can be played with a foot pedal, the hands are left free to play on other instruments.

But there are several disadvantages, though some may be overcome if instructions are written into the score. Bass drums in jazz sets may be too small for concert use, and their internal dampers make for short sounds which may be unsuitable. These dampers would have to be removed. Also, though the foot pedal can be used with precision over a fair dynamic range and to give both staccato and 'long' notes, it can by no means equal the touch and dynamics of normal stick technique; and of course a pedal roll is impossible. However, drum sticks can always be used if the hands are not otherwise employed.

Tambourine

This is a frame drum consisting of a wooden hoop with a single skin lapped over one edge and nailed into position. In addition, the frame is usually slotted and fitted with pairs of small round cymbals or 'jingles'. Tambourines without jingles are sometimes included in scores (e.g. Falla's *El Retablo de Maese Pedro*), but this is rare. Normally, it is the jingle sound that composers require, rather than the drum sound.

Modern instruments are usually between 8 and 12 in. (20 and 30 cm.) in diameter and are fitted with a large number of jingles. Though the tambourine has often been used to evoke a Neapolitan or Spanish atmosphere, it need not be associated with such local colours. Its genius is to give zest and a festive spirit to music of a lively character, though it is now often used for other delicate and more abstract effects.

The instrument may be played in several ways:

(*a*) It may be shaken in one hand to give a 'jingle roll', indicated by the tremolo sign and the word 'shake'.

(*b*) Holding the instrument in one hand, the vellum is struck by the fingers, knuckles or palm of the other hand, or the instrument is struck against the knee. These are the normal ways of playing single strokes, repeated-note rhythms, etc.

(*c*) The instrument may be laid on a cushion either way up, and played with the fingers or with drumsticks.

(*d*) A 'thumb roll' may be produced by rubbing a moistened thumb across the vellum. This gives a quiet jingle trill of short duration. Indicate by tremolo signs and the word 'thumb'. This is most suitable for very soft trills or sudden crescendos, but the repeated forte use of this effect in some scores is impossible to play.

The tambourine can produce a wide range of effects with fine dynamic graduations, and these should be carefully notated. For example:

Ex. 119   Stockhausen: *Gruppen*

The following example contains a synthesis of various effects:

Ex. 120

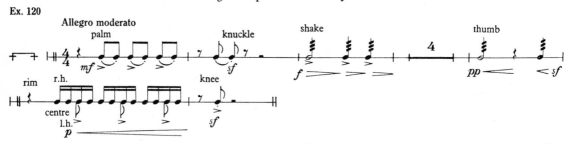

The tambourine without jingles is common in Italy, where it is called 'tamburello'. The Orff-Schulwerk includes 'tambours' of similar type. Their single head has tensioning screws and they range from 10 to 20 in. (26 to 50 cm.) in diameter. The sound is surprisingly deep and resonant for such simple instruments.

Provençal Tambourine

This is a tall 'tabor' about a metre long, double-headed, and with a snare on the batter head. The player uses his right hand to beat out a continuous ostinato, while with his left, he plays on a simple pipe. It is used in the folk music of Southern France and Northern Spain.

African Drum

Though examples of all the four main types of drum (single-skin, double-skin, frame drum, and friction drum) are found in so many forms in Africa, the 'African drum' occasionally used in Western music is the single-headed, cup-shaped or goblet drum.

Though the shape and size may vary, the most common type is made with a wooden shell deeper than the diameter of the skin. The upper half of the shell is cylindrical, the lower part is of slightly conical shape—hence the term 'goblet drum'.

The single skin is tautened by a large number of tension cords which run down the sides of the shell to a shoulder formed at the division of the cylindrical and conic shapes of the two halves of the shell. The tension cords are passed under a hoop of circular rope which fits below this shoulder.

The drum is played with the hands or with hook-shaped sticks, and players can obtain a variety of suggestive effects including modulations of timbre and sounds of varying pitch.

Chinese Drum

Again, there are many forms of Chinese drums, but the type usually referred to in Western music is a small double-skinned drum about 9 to 18 in. (23 to 46 cm.) in diameter and 4 to 6 in. (10 to 15 cm.) deep. The shell is made of thick wood and is slightly rounded in its depth.

The skins are fixed by nails, and are usually covered with decorative paintings. The layers of paint thicken the skins so that these instruments may have a sound unusually deep and resonant for such small drums.

The drum is suspended by a ring fixed to the shell and may be played by the hands, or with timpani sticks.

TIMPANI. TABLAS. BOOBAMS

Timpani or Kettledrums

Although ancient in origin, timpani were only made suitable for orchestral use in the seventeenth century, when screw tensioning devices were invented for tightening and tuning the heads. During the last hundred years, various mechanisms have been invented for tuning timpani quickly and accurately by means of a single hand-screw or foot pedal, or by turning the whole drum on a pivot incorporating a tensioning screw. Timpani fitted with these rapid tuning devices are generically called 'machine drums'. Revolving drums have been popular on the Continent, while drums with a single master handle are coming into use where economy is important (as in school orchestras). But the most favoured machine drum is the foot pedal model.

Pedal timpani are more useful than other machine drums because changes of pitch can be done rapidly without using the hands. They are by now standard equipment in most symphony orchestras, though often hand-tuned timpani have been retained as auxiliary instruments. When scoring for professional orchestras it is safe to assume that pedal timpani will be available. But for amateur orchestras it is best to restrict the parts to what can be played on two hand-tuned drums.

Timpani sizes

Timpani are made in various sizes, and each size is most suited to a certain pitch range. Though makers may proudly advertise that 'a full octave is easily obtainable on each instrument', the best tone of a drum is within a limited zone. If the head is tautened beyond this, to obtain higher notes, its elasticity is reduced and the drum will sound 'knocky' and toneless. With the head too slack (for low notes) the tone again deteriorates, with the added disadvantage of pitch distortion. When low notes are attacked forcibly, the vellum stretches, the notes sound flat and then 'scoop' up to pitch as the head returns to its normal shape. The lowest notes of timpani tend to be indefinite in pitch.

Timpani are usually available in four sizes—30, 28, 25, and 23 in. (78, 71, 64, and 57 cm.) in diameter. If only two instruments are employed they are normally the 28 and 25 in. (71 and 64 cm.) sizes, and are used to play sounds within the octave F to *f*. Each drum is regarded as having a pitch range of a perfect fifth:

Ex. 121

These pitch ranges are so devised that three notes can be played on either drum (B flat, B natural, and C), so that a second sound can be obtained either above or below, as necessary.

The 23 and 30 in. (57 and 78 cm.) drums are used to extend this range a third upwards and downwards, to give a compass of one twelfth from D to *a*, though it is best to avoid the extreme notes. For low notes down to C sharp, a 32 in (83 cm.) drum is used. If four timpani are scored for, they should normally have the following pitch ranges:

Ex. 122

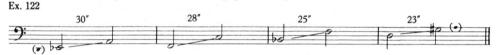

Most large orchestras now possess a small drum, called 'piccolo timpano', which is used for high notes. The range is from *f* to *c*, so bringing the possible timpani sounds up to middle C.

Naturally, if only three timpani are scored for, (they are adequate for all but exceptional circumstances), a decision must be made at the outset as to whether the 23 or 30 in. drum will be most suitable to add to the 'middle' pair.

If each drum is to be used at or near its best tension, it must be borne in mind that their 'mean' tension will give pitches near the following four notes:

Ex. 123

By altering these tunings only a semitone in one direction or a tone in the other, it is possible to form a complete chromatic scale of notes from low E to top *g*:

Ex. 124

(mean notes)

If timpani are used with this tuning plan, good tone will always result. In addition, pitch changes on hand-tuned drums can easily be accomplished, for the maximum alteration of tuning required on any drum is only a minor third.

It would be impossible to restrict every timpani part to the above tuning plan. For example, it eliminates the possibility of scale passages altogether, while many passages which include semitones are excluded (e.g. A, B flat, D, C sharp) unless the drums are altered in pitch between notes—which may not always be convenient or satisfactory. However, as timpani sound best, and their different pitches are more evident, when their sounds are kept some distance apart, it will be found that the above tuning plan will answer most purposes.

It must be stressed that the number of drums to be scored for, and their sizes, must be decided on at an early stage in the composition.

Positioning of drums

Timpani are played with the larger drums on the left and the smallest on the right, so that their sounds are in ascending pitch order from left to right. (In Germany this order is reversed.) Where there are more than two timpani, the instruments are arranged in a half circle round the player, so that each instrument is as nearly as possible the same distance from the player's body.

Timpani may be played in a standing position, or the player may prefer to be seated on a stool. A semi-sitting position is favoured when using pedal timpani, so that two pedals can be manipulated at the same time.

Timpani sticks

These are available in three degrees of hardness according to whether the core is covered with soft, medium, or hard felt. Some sticks have double ends. In addition to the felt heads, they have wood ball-or pear-shaped ends, so that the sticks may be quickly reversed. Naturally different sticks influence the tone, attack, and volume of sounds considerably.

In general, players can be left to make their own choice of sticks. Timpanists are usually highly individual personalities, and in fact may well ignore a composer's indications. However, where the general timbre, volume, and attack require a particular kind of stick, this can certainly be indicated.

'Sponge' sticks are sometimes indicated by composers. But they should be avoided, as the soft ball end spreads on contact with the vellum and damps the tone.

Timpani may be played with snare drum sticks, producing brilliant staccato sounds which can be obtained in no other way. Naturally the tone is hard and thin and there is a fair degree of contact sound, but these factors may be ideal for certain musical situations, and have certainly found favour with composers of the stature of Bartók, Stravinsky, and Britten. Some timpanists of the old school, with their own ideals of tone, resist this style of playing, and there is in fact some danger of damaging the vellum when snare drum sticks are used too forcibly. For this reason, snare drum sticks should not be indicated in forte passages, but simply 'wooden sticks'. In this case the player will use timpani sticks with a wooden ball at the end, which will not spoil the vellums. However, as snare drum sticks can produce very crisp, light tones, one should not hesitate to specify them for lighter passages where energy and verve are wanted, rather than volume. (Timpanists seem to have different opinions about the use of snare drum sticks. Some expert players say a vellum will only be damaged by snare drum sticks through defective strokes, that is, hammering strokes, rather than the correct 'whip' (rebounding) strokes.)

Other methods of striking
Light rolls or single strokes are occasionally played with a couple of coins (pennies or half-crowns) or even the fingernails.

In chamber ensembles, composers are introducing finger playing, which has such a wide range of possibilities in light textures. Certainly finger-style playing permits much finer grades of quiet dynamics than normal techniques, and allows the effective use of timpani at a volume scale which is ideally suited to chamber music.

There are many unconventional ways of striking timpani indicated in modern scores (e.g. with wire brushes, metal sticks, triangle beaters, knife blades, and even with maracas), but none of these has produced effects of notable value. The same is true of such oddities as playing on the rim or shell of the instrument.

The beating spot
Timpani are normally struck at a point three or four inches from the rim. At this 'beating spot', the fullest tone is produced, the pitch is most defined, and the sound most sustained. If the drum is struck between the beating spot and the centre these characteristics disappear as the centre is approached, until at the middle of the drum only a short dead thud is emitted. Composers have occasionally indicated single strokes or rolls at the centre of a drum when an indeterminate, colourless sound has been desired.

When struck between the beating spot and the rim, the tone thins down as the rim is approached. This effect can be accentuated if wooden sticks are used, producing a brittle sound much in contrast with the timpani's usually mellow 'boom'.

It follows that it is possible for a player to produce on the same drum, and with the same pair of beaters, quite a range of different sounds. In the past the ideal has been always one of unity of timbre and exact pitch definition, so that any unorthodox usage has been avoided. In the future, such ideals may not always prevail, and a timpani's different tones may be exploited more.

Damping and Muting

Timpani sounds have a sustained quality, and ring on for some time after they are struck. This 'ring' can be most objectionable where it is not wanted, and is prevented by 'finger damping', the player touching the drum skins gently with the three free fingers of either hand. At times the music moves so quickly that finger damping between notes is not possible. In this case the ring of the drums can be reduced by placing cloth or felt pads on the vellum, which is also the method of muting the drums.

Tuning

We have no need to consider the tuning of timpani before a movement begins, but it is important to realize the problems of re-tuning once the music is under way.

When changing the pitch of a hand-tuned drum, the player usually turns the handle nearest to him, then the nearest handles on each side simultaneously, and then goes round the drum in a similar manner. If the change of pitch is large, he will probably repeat this process several times, so as to keep the vellum evenly tensioned all over, changing the pitch by even steps.

With hand-tuned drums it is therefore advisable to:

(1) Allow at least ten seconds for an accurate change of pitch of up to a tone, and proportionately longer for larger intervals. This time-period is to be recommended where professional players are not available. A good timpanist can re-tune in half this time.

(2) Keep changes of pitch to small intervals wherever possible.

With pedal timpani, alterations of pitch can be done very quickly. The pedal is light in action, can be moved rapidly and a large alteration in pitch can be accomplished just as quickly as a small one. Tuning gauges are now quite accurate. But though it is possible to play a quick succession of different sounds on a single pedal drum, one must beware of introducing glissando effects where they are not wanted. If a drum skin is altered in tension too soon after it is sounded, the note will scoop up or down to the next tuning, unless the sound is damped before the pedal is moved. Time must therefore be allowed for the note to be damped, or its sound to die away sufficiently, before the pedal needs to be moved. This is particularly necessary when the alteration in tuning is a large interval. With a tuning gauge, successions of notes which involve re-tuning by large intervals can in fact be played as rapidly as the notes can be struck and damped. It would be quite safe to write such re-tunings for professional players in quarter notes at $\quarternote = 72$, or faster. (Some professionals use a pedalling technique in which the pedal is moved only as the stick descends to strike. Foot and hand are synchronized in such a way that successions of different notes can be played quickly, without damping being necessary.)

Small steps do not need damping and can be written at a moderate speed without glissando effects becoming too evident, as in the following successions of semitones:

Many professionals would prefer to play the above passage on no more than three drums, the reason being that the sympathetic vibrations on five drums are difficult to control. In fact many good players prefer to use only two timpani whenever possible, for the same reason.

Tuning indications

Sometimes composers give no indications whatsoever as to how many timpani are to be used, nor how they are to be tuned or re-tuned. For instance, even so meticulous a composer as Bartók gave no information as to how many drums are required in his Concerto for Orchestra, nor how they should be tuned for the following passage:

In these few bars there are ten different notes and seven changes of metre. Obviously this can only be played with some preparation. The player must study his part before a rehearsal and mark all re-tunings, deciding which drum is to be used for each note.

But in these days of limited rehearsal time, good results cannot be obtained unless players are given every assistance possible, by solving their problems beforehand. The composer or arranger should therefore think out all performing details himself. (In any case, parts can never be well written for instruments unless performing problems are solved as the notes are put on paper.)

There is no standard way of indicating re-tunings, and there is some difference of opinion as to how they should be written. One thing is certain, however: re-tuning indications should be shown *as early as possible*. They should be included in the drum part as soon as the player is free to re-tune, not just before he next begins to play.

For a long time, composers have shown re-tunings as follows: 'Change E to F, D to C♯' etc. This worked very well as long as re-tunings were infrequent, the number of timpani were few (so that there was no doubt as to which was referred to) and the change of interval small.

For re-tunings between phrases this system can still be used. It is preferable to show which drum is referred to by using roman numerals. Drums should be numbered from left to right, the lowest being 'I'. This is the method usually employed and seems most logical, as we are accustomed to count from the left. However, many composers number the drums from right to left.

The indications should be grouped vertically, for example:

$$\begin{array}{ll} \text{IV} & \text{F♯—G} \\ \text{III} & \text{D—E♭} \\ \text{II} & \text{B♭—B♮} \\ \text{I} & \text{G—F} \end{array}$$

Sometimes when a re-tuning involves a large change of pitch there can be doubt as to whether this is upwards or downwards. This should be clarified as follows:

$$\begin{array}{ll} \text{III} & \text{C♯ ↗ high F♯} \\ \text{II} & \text{B ↘ low F} \end{array}$$

An alternative method, which has the advantage of great clarity and simplicity, can be illustrated without any explanation. Here are various successive tunings of four timpani:

$$\boxed{\text{E G♯ C F}} \rightarrow \boxed{\text{— A — —}} \rightarrow \boxed{\text{F — — E}}$$

One can see at a glance that the first re-tuning concerns only drum II and the next drums I and IV.

Unfortunately this method only shows the *new* pitches. To find the *previous* tunings (if they are not remembered) the player has to look back at previous 'rectangles'. However, the rectangles can be written large, so that they stand out like milestones in the music, providing a very clear picture of the tuning plan.

Unfortunately, both the previous tuning indications take up too much space where re-tunings are frequent. In this case it is best to keep to the very simple method shown in the next example, in which the previously quoted passage from Bartók's Concerto is written out for three pedal timpani (30, 28, and 25 in.):

Ex. 127

Bartók: *Concerto for Orchestra*

The brackets indicate the tuning progressions for each drum, the Roman numerals show which timpani are used. In addition, some re-tunings may be shown by arrows pointing up or down to the new note. This is sometimes necessary where re-tunings are far apart and not bracketed. For example, drum I is not used after the F in bar 5 until the final G. This alteration from F up to G is shown with an arrow pointing upwards in bar 5. The other two arrowed indications are not quite so necessary, but are nonetheless helpful.

No single system of tuning indications is perfect in itself. But one method can be used to supplement another, so that the timpanist has a maximum of assistance. For instance, Chou Wen-Chung, who seems to be the composer with the most meticulously detailed timpani parts, uses more than one system within a single composition.

The true pitch of timpani sounds

Timpani are almost universally regarded as sounding at the written pitch. But some musicians of considerable repute affirm that the true sound is an octave lower than that written.

Certainly it seems probable that the real fundamental tone of timpani is an octave lower than written pitch. This can be deduced from the fact that a timpani sound usually comprises two prominent tones, a fifth apart, the lowest one being that written, the other being a strong overtone. As a fundamental tone cannot have an overtone only a fifth higher, it seems impossible that the lowest sound (at written pitch) is the true fundamental. As first and second overtones are higher, at the octave and the twelfth, it therefore seems certain that the above two sounds, a fifth apart, are in fact the first and second overtones of a fundamental which is not clearly audible, or is only audible to some very perceptive ears.

The author's own experience is that if a beating spot on the drum head is found which elicits as few high overtones as possible, a gentle stroke with a soft beater will reveal a deep sound. Though this sound is not very distinct (probably being disturbed by differential tones), it certainly appears to be an octave lower than written pitch, and must be the true fundamental tone.

However, it seems an indisputable fact that for most of us timpani have their most prominent sounds at the written pitch, so there is absolutely no point in writing the sounds an octave lower, at the pitch of the largely inaudible fundamentals.

Before leaving this section, it is opportune to mention that the timpani overtone a fifth higher than written pitch can sometimes cause unhappy effects. For instance, in Toscanini's recording of the first prelude in *Parsifal*, at the *Motif des Glaubens* (played forte at first by two trumpets and horn), when the timpani interrupts with a low E flat (the harmonic bass) it sounds like a B flat. So the harmony, instead of sounding in root position, seems to be a second inversion. This kind of effect is heard frequently enough (especially when hard beaters are used in a forte passage), but there is little one can do to eliminate it.

Basic Timpani Strokes

Single Strokes

Timpani are normally played with *alternating strokes* of each stick. When moving from a low drum to a higher one, the left hand begins when there are an odd number of notes before the move, while for even-numbered groups, the right hand begins:

Ex. 128

Moving from a high drum to a low one, the order is reversed. The right hand begins odd-numbered groups of notes and the left hand even-numbered ones.

Cross-over beats

When passing from one drum to another, cross-over beats are sometimes unavoidable:

Ex. 129   Kelemen: *Équilibres*

Whether this passage is begun with the left or right stick, the hands must cross to play the first F sharp.

Cross-overs are a special feature in timpani-playing. They look well, and need not be avoided in normal circumstances. But when the music is rapid and the number of timpani used is more than three, they can get players into a tangle. For instance, the following passage for five timpani is full of rapid cross-overs, which are made particularly difficult because of the distance between the outside drums (note the cross-overs between drum I and V at 'x' and 'y'):

Ex. 130
Parris: *Concerto for Five Kettledrums and Orchestra*

It is worth noting that an inconvenient cross-over in rapid phrases can be eliminated by repeating a note just before the 'cross'. The repeated C in the following passage allows the phrase to be played with alternating beats without crossing hands:

Ex. 131
Kelemen: *Équilibres*

Difficult cross-overs are sometimes eliminated by setting up the timpani in a special order for a particular piece.

Double beats

Though it is preferable for timpani always to be played with alternating strokes, it is often necessary to introduce a double beat with one hand or the other in order to avoid a profusion of cross-over beats. For example, if the following passage were to be played hand-to-hand two cross-overs would be unavoidable, and at speed these could prove quite awkward. But with left-hand double beats (as shown), the passage has no difficulties.

Ex. 132

Sometimes double beats take the form of the 'paradiddle', which is particularly useful in avoiding cross-overs in passages of rapidly repeated notes:

Ex. 133

The roll

Timpani rolls are played with single alternating strokes, not with the rebounding 'daddy-mammy' technique of the side drum. Once the roll is begun, the drum's vibrations mount up to a sustained tone, so that the separate strokes are not obvious. However, separate strokes can become too apparent at pianissimo on high notes, so some players prefer rebounding strokes in these circumstances.

Timpani rolls are almost always written as trills, except for the rolls on two or more drums mentioned below. Care must be taken to indicate the exact duration of the roll, and how it should end (either on an accented note, or without any accent).

Rolls can include wide contrasts of volume, and such dynamic contrasts can be exploited with great effect, providing of course that they suit the musical situation.

For example:

Ex. 134

Double rolls can be performed on two drums, and should be written as at (*a*) below. Rolls on three and four drums are also possible with two sticks in one or both hands, as at (*b*) and (*c*) in the following example:

Ex. 135

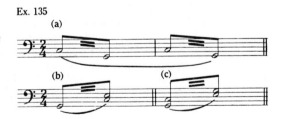

Embellishments

Decorations are very rarely seen in timpani parts. Certainly they cannot have the clarity of grace notes and other embellishments as played on the snare drum. Nor is the flourish and snap of decorative drum beats much in harmony with the sober character of timpani.

However, embellishments could probably be used more frequently than is the present custom, particularly in those passages where wooden sticks are used for crisp, staccato effects. The following is an example of the use of the flam and open drag (played with wooden sticks) in a recurring timpani solo in Chou Wen-Chung's *All in the Spring Wind*. It is instructive to note how much less significant this brief solo would be without the embellishments:

Ex. 136   Chou Wen-Chung: *All in the Spring Wind*

f (wooden sticks)

Naturally, drags and ruffs must be open, played with light hand-to-hand strokes before a down stroke. Do not write slurs with these embellishments.

The glissando

This is the most prominent expressive effect introduced by pedal timpani. It is performed by moving the pedal after the drum is struck, so that the intonation scoops to a new note (higher or lower) in a given time period. Glissandos can be up or down. Upward glissandos are more effective, because the drum retains its sonority better when the skin is tightened. When it is slackened for downward glissandos, the volume of sound falls off quickly. Either upward or downward glissandos can be rolled, in which case, of course, the volume is sustained throughout.

Glissandos can span up to an octave, providing they begin at the upper or lower limit of the instrument's compass. From the middle of a drum's range, the glissando can naturally be no more than a diminished fifth at most. However, glissandos are rarely written over a range of more than a major sixth, while smaller intervals are much more common. The following example shows various single-stroked and rolled glissandos and the method of notation:

Ex. 137
(a)   (b)   (c)

In (*a*) are shown single-stroke glissandos. As a slur is written between the notes of each glissando, the final ones will not be sounded by separate strokes.

On the other hand, (*b*) shows separate strokes for the notes beginning and ending each glissando, (the final notes can often be played with advantage on a separate drum), whilst (*c*) shows rolled glissandos, first rising a minor third, and then descending by semitone steps. There is no glissando between the E flat and D.

Composers frequently use the tremolo sign for glissando rolls, or when brief rolls are separated by other notes. Certainly the use of the tremolo sign is to be recommended where space is limited and where it is important to show the duration of rolls with precision.

For example:

Ex. 138

Chords

Two-note chords are performed by striking two drums simultaneously, and may be placed among single-note groupings to give accentuations:

Ex. 139

♪ = 252   F♯ B C

Daniel Jones: *Sonata*

(*ff*)

Three- and four-note chords are also possible, and can be played with greater precision in the hands of a single player (but with less force) than when a number of players are used. For example, a passage such as the following (using first three and then four sticks) can be played by a single timpanist with ease:

Ex. 140 F B♭ D G

With pedal timpani, two-note chords can be played with various tunings, though it is naturally easier for the player if retunings are simple and straight-forward, as in the following example of parallel motion:

Ex. 141 III

♪=72 I

Parris: *Concerto for Five Kettledrums and Orchestra*

Where force and attack are required, *doubled notes* can be played on one drum with both sticks. This is best indicated by writing stems above and below each note.

Sharp colour contrasts

Colours obtained with the various sticks have already been discussed, as also alterations in tone obtained by striking the head at points other than the normal 'beating spot'. These different timbres are not usually varied rapidly. However, well-defined contrasts of colour are sometimes required within a phrase, and these may be obtained by using different sticks in each hand. In the Farbermann Concerto quotation shown in Ex. 125 all sforzando notes are required to be played with a wooden stick in the left hand, the remainder being played by a felt-headed stick in the right.

Double-headed sticks, with wooden ball ends as well as felt, are very use-ful for obtaining rapid alterations of tone, as they can be reversed very quickly. In the following example, both ends of left- and right-hand sticks are used, in each case the reversal taking place within the space of two quavers (a little less than one second).

turn left stick to wood end

Ex. 142

(♩ = 62–65)

Farberman: *Concerto for Timpani and Orchestra*

★turn right stick to wood end

mf L L L L L R   R L   L L R R R R

★turn to felt side

In the following example, hard felt sticks are used in each hand, but timbre contrasts are obtained by striking some notes near the rim. The rim notes (marked 'R') will have a hard tone and will probably 'knock':

Ex. 143
♩ = 96
Cowell: *Concerto for Percussion and Orchestra*

f (hard sticks)   normal

Orchestral Use of the Timpani

Timpani have been and still are, the most-used percussion instruments in the orchestra. They are almost always to be found in scores requiring large forces, and are often present in those for smaller ensembles. This frequent use of the instruments points to a wider range of functions than the noise-making 'dynamic reinforcement of the orchestral tutti' given as timpani's main role in some orchestration books. There is no doubt that dynamic reinforcement is a very prominent role for these instruments, but they have many other uses as well. The following sections sum up the most prominent functions of timpani, but cannot pretend to be completely exhaustive.

(1) *Melody*

Solo melodies using scale patterns are seldom found in timpani parts, and rapid successions of tones and semitones as in Ex. 143 are quite unusual.

Composers have probably avoided solo melodies with such scalewise patterns for two reasons. Firstly, unless the melody is to be very limited in scope, a large number of timpani must be used, or re-tunings must be very frequent. In the Cowell Concerto quoted in Ex. 143, eight hand-tuned drums are scored for, or a minimum of five pedal timpani. Secondly, scale-type melodies require each note to be perfectly in tune and *precisely defined in pitch*. Though timpani can be accurately tuned, they have less pitch definition than any other bass instrument in the orchestra. Adjacent notes are thus not readily distinguishable one from the other. Solo melodic passages for timpani are therefore mostly based on a pattern of a few well-separated notes, which are often enough the components of a chord:

Ex. 144   G C E
Moderato   (felt sticks)   Britten: *The Young Person's Guide to the Orchestra*

mf distinto

Very often, solos are based on repetitions of a melodic cell, such as the following pattern in Hindemith's *Sinfonische Metamorphosen*. Such recurring figures are particularly suited to the genius of the instruments:

Ex. 145

Hindemith: *Sinfonische Metamorphosen*

Sometimes a brief timpani solo is used to 'clinch' a moment of dynamic or rhythmic culmination:

Ex. 146

Gunther Schuller: *Symphony for Brass and Percussion*

Note, in the last three examples of timpani solos, how the drums are tuned well apart so as to obtain a distinct *pitch differentiation*.

So far, this section has only dealt with melody for timpani solo. Much more frequently however, timpani are doubled by other bass instruments. As these define the pitch of the sounds adequately, and lend definition to the timpani notes, there is no longer any need for pre-occupation on this score. Any succession of notes can be written, providing of course that they are playable. The timpani melody in the following example, for instance, uses successions of adjacent notes which one would certainly avoid if the drums were solo, but here the function of the timpani is to give punch and drive to the melody. The passage is written for two timpanists with hand-tuned drums, but could be performed by a single player, with or without pedal timpani:

Ex. 147   Holst: *The Planets*

(2) *Dynamic reinforcement*

The reinforcement of orchestral dynamics has two main aspects, which are
not always recognized as being quite separate and distinct. One is concerned
with *accentuation*, the other with *volume*. That these are really quite different
factors can be readily appreciated if one thinks how it is quite possible to have
accentuation without loudness, and sheer volume without any accentuation.
Admittedly, the two often go together (especially in timpani parts!). But it is
important to realize that they are not always the same thing.

Rolls usually serve for gradations in volume, and groups of single strokes
for accentuation. But this is only a generalization, not a rule. For single strokes
can certainly produce alterations in volume, and rolls can give a degree of
accentuation. This is shown in the following example. In the first two bars,
the single timpani strokes (each with a closed drag) serve to punctuate the
beats with a clear accentuation, but at the same time they underline the
prominent crescendo. The timpani roll in the last three bars produces
alterations in volume, and in addition, supports the sforzandos in other parts.

Ex. 148

Britten: *The Young Person's Guide to the Orchestra*

Note, by the way, how timpani notes are ready to blend with different sounds whenever possible. In the last three bars in this example the real bass note is D flat, but the timpani do not need to be retuned, as F is part of the harmony. Naturally, it would be preferable if timpani could always play the same notes as the orchestral bass, but when this is not possible, they can be given notes which have a close harmonic relationship to it.

(3) *Ostinatos*

Timpani are very effective in playing rhythmic ostinatos which serve as a foundation for different material played by other instruments. The following example shows the timpani ostinato in Alan Hovhaness's Symphony No. 8, which runs through many parts of the work's single movement, thus serving as a unifying factor. The ostinato, with its nervous restlessness, is in contrast to the sustained, noble character of the other thematic material, played in canon:

Ex. 149   Alan Hovhaness: *Symphony No. 8*

This use of timpani in opposition to the rest of the orchestra is very effective, particularly in loud incisive passages such as the following:

Ex. 150   Heimo Erbse: *Pavimento*

(4) *Background colour*

Soft rolls on the timpani give a mysterious, shuddering quality to quiet orchestral harmonies:

Ex. 151   Britten: *Peter Grimes*

Isolated notes or short trills give an impression of solemnity, darkness, or an ominous atmosphere:

Ex. 152   Bartók: *Music for Strings, Percussion and Celesta*

(5) *Timpani as an orchestral bass*

Timpani can be used as an orchestral bass, though due to their lack of a strong degree of pitch definition, they are seldom used solo for this purpose. However, where the harmony is already well evident, there is no reason why timpani cannot be used as a bass without support from any other instrument. For example:

Ex. 153   Cowell: *Concerto for Percussion and Orchestra*

The 'moderato assai' of Tchaikovsky's Fourth Symphony contains another well-known example of the timpani as a solo bass to upper string and woodwind parts. The volume is pianissimo and the timpani give an attractive lilt to this gentle music.[1] Much more frequently, however, some other instrument joins with the timpani to give the sounds a firm intonation. In quiet music this is best done by instruments which blend well with the timpani, such as double bass pizzicato, the piano, harp, or bass clarinet.

One of Stravinsky's favourite devices is to use the kettledrums as a bass with as little support from other instruments as possible. In the following example from *Agon* the timpani are supported by the harp, below a quiet texture of double-bass harmonics and flutes:

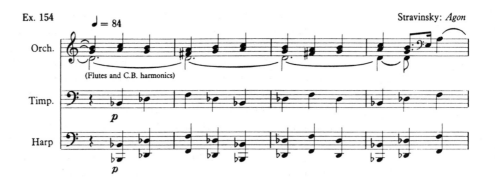

Ex. 154   Stravinsky: *Agon*

It should be noted in this example that while the upper parts are in G major, the bass is in B flat minor—a simple example of 'bitonality'. For this contrast in tonalities to be made apparent, it is therefore all the more necessary for the bass to be clearly defined—so the addition of the harp is quite essential.

(6) *Timpani as untuned percussion*

During this century, music has become highly chromatic. So much so that with some compositional techniques such as serialism, free atonalism or free twelve-note writing, the total-chromatic of twelve different semitones is in constant use. Contrary to the practice in tonal music of using only notes of

---

[1] Note in this score the old practice of writing timpani parts without key signatures and omitting accidentals in the parts. Accidentals were only indicated at re-tunings. On page 25 of Boosey and Hawkes miniature score, it will be seen that erroneous retuning indications, and the lack of key signatures and accidentals, create a confusing situation. Obviously, key signatures and all accidentals should always be written, as for other instruments.

the diatonic scale, and dwelling on certain of these in such a way as to emphasize key centres, the new music avoids sensations of 'key' by constantly contradicting tonal implications. This means that all the twelve available semitones recur constantly over short time periods.

This has posed serious problems in scoring for timpani, particularly before pedal drums were common, as such chromatic music implies constant re-tunings. One solution adopted has been to use the timpani as little as possible. Webern hardly scored for them at all. Schoenberg used timpani in a hesitant way. For example, his serial Variations for Orchestra is a work of massive orchestral forces, yet right up to the finale the timpanist only plays twenty-four strokes. In more recent times, composers of stature such as Stockhausen and Messiaen seem to have avoided using timpani even in works of massive sonority.

Even since pedal timpani have become common, there are still problems. For example, in *Il Canto Sospeso* Luigi Nono requires re-tunings for almost every new note in timpani parts which have very complex rhythmic problems. To ease the difficulties he uses three players. Even so, the use of the instruments is very limited indeed for music of such forceful character.

It would seem that if timpani are to be re-tuned for almost every note, their use is going to be too restricted. But there is a very simple solution. In serial music (and in music using similar techniques), the re-tuning of timpani can be avoided by giving them certain fixed notes in a certain passage and omitting these notes from other instrumental parts. The use of the total-chromatic is maintained and there is no need to re-tune. When a suitable rest occurs, the timpanist can re-tune for the next 'fixed-note' passage, and so on.

But there is a still more common-sense solution. That is, to maintain the same tunings over long periods, thus virtually treating timpani as instruments of indefinite pitch. Unless supported at the unison by other instruments, their sounds are in any case not sufficiently defined in pitch to be distinctly heard in a mass of complex sounds. In ultra-chromatic music, too, when notes are scattered in profusion like grains of wheat on the threshing floor, their individual values are so transient that no single note seems particularly important. So why demand any specific sounds from timpani?

Some composers have taken the decisive step of writing for timpani as 'untuned percussion'. Though tunings are given, this is only to ensure sounds within certain pitch zones, i.e. high notes, low notes, and so on. For example, in his *Transfigurationen*, Milko Kelemen uses two timpani almost continuously in the last fifty bars of the work, always tuned to low F sharp and high F natural. The music is highly chromatic, and in such an example as the following, it is obvious that the timpani notes have no other pitch significance than merely high and low percussive sounds:

Ex. 155   Milko Kelemen: *Transfigurationen*

The truth is that timpani are only one degree more defined in pitch than some other drums (particularly tomtoms), and the ear can accept them as instruments of either definite or indefinite pitch according to circumstances. One of these circumstances is certainly an atonal context.

In his *Creation Epic* for orchestra, the author made an experiment. Three timpani were always tuned to the same high, medium, and low sounds and were written for as untuned percussion, just like the eight other drums used in this work (see Exx. 177 and 178). It was found that in performance, the ear accepts the timpani notes as sounds of indefinite pitch, and is not disturbed by clashes between timpani sounds and notes played by the bass instruments of the orchestra. If instead, an attempt had been made to give timpani sounds pitch significance, the problems of re-tuning would have been so formidable as to reduce their use to only a fraction of what has in fact been possible.

Conclusion

One last word on timpani. It is important to remember that they have long melodious sounds as a primary characteristic. So they are not suited to rapid passages. Though timpani can be played rapidly, the sounds will not be sharp and clean, but will tend to merge together into a booming roar which may be the very opposite of the rapid, staccato effect the composer probably intended. This is particularly so when a large number of instruments are used, as in rapid passages the player has no time to damp out unwanted sounds (including sympathetic vibrations). If rapid drum sounds are essential the composer would do well to consider the use of smaller drums, such as tomtoms, with their shorter, more staccato sounds, and brighter, more incisive tone.

Lastly, it is best to use as few timpani as possible, so that though more pedalling may be required, the tones of the instruments may be more easily controlled.

Tabla

The tabla is an oriental drum found in various forms over a wide area. As far as we are concerned, there are two main kinds of tabla—that used in India and that found, with slight variations of form, in most Arabic countries. The Indian and Arabic tablas are quite different, though Western composers often fail to indicate which type of tabla they require.

The *Indian tabla* is a small single-headed drum with a completely closed resonating chamber. Sometimes, with larger instruments, the shell is made of metal in a bowl-shaped form resembling that of timpani. Smaller tablas have thick wooden cylindrical shells, the bottom aperture being closed by a heavy wooden stopper. The characteristic feature of this type of tabla is the way the single membrane is tautened by long tensioning straps which stretch vertically from top to bottom of the instrument every couple of inches all round the drum. Cylindrical pieces of wood are inserted between the straps and the shell, and by moving these up and down, the straps may be tautened or slackened, so that the drum-head can be finely tuned.

The Indian tabla has a mellow, round, sustained sound of very musical character and well-defined pitch, rather like that of timpani. In fact, these instruments can be regarded as a form of high-pitched kettledrum, and Western composers have so far written music for them which brings out the characteristically well-tuned, long-sustained sound of the instrument. Soft dynamics are preferred in order to preserve the instrument's mellow tones, and the tablas are played with soft-headed timpani sticks. Up to twelve tablas have been used, so as to obtain a chromatic octave of sounds in the middle register.

However, authentic Indian tabla playing is quite a different matter. It is a highly trained profession. The player uses every joint and knuckle of his fingers and thumbs to produce a wide vocabulary of sounds, and every part of the drum skin is made to give out its particular tones. In fact these drums are made to talk in a way which is quite beyond the possibilities of a Western performer—there is no point in our trying to imitate Indian tabla techniques with a pair of drumsticks! However, these instruments are obviously well suited to producing sounds of varied pitch and tone colour, and well merit further attention from composers and further experimentation by performers. (For Indian drum techniques the reader is referred to the Philips recording *Song and Sound the World Around—India*, on which are recorded sounds of the Indian Dhol, Anandalahari, and Tablas. Authentic Indian instruments may be obtained from the Lahore Music House, Darya Ganj, Delhi-6, India.)

The *Arabic tabla* has a mushroom or egg-cup shape. The drum's membrane is stretched across a broad, shallow, cup-shaped shell, which then continues downwards in a thinner leg, which may be cylindrical, or broaden out to a bell-like orifice. The bottom of the 'leg' is always open.

In Morocco, Tunisia, and Algeria, tabla shells are usually made of earthenware. In Iran they are usually wooden, while in Syria, the Lebanon, and Turkey, they are metal. The membrane can always be tuned, either by tension thongs, or (in the case of metal shells) with thumb screws. Examples of Arabic tablas are to be found in oriental shops. A version of the Turkish tabla or 'dumbeg' is made by the American Rawhide Manufacturing Co., 1103 North Branch St., Chicago 22, Illinois.

The Arabic tabla is normally laid horizontally across the left knee, but may sometimes be held under the left arm. In the latter case the drum-skin is beaten with both hands, the left hand beating near the rim to produce high, bright tones, while the right hand beats the centre of the skin to obtain deeper, dark sounds.

When the tabla is laid across the left knee, the left hand can be introduced into the open end of the shell 'leg', so that sounds of different pitch can be produced by moving the hand up and down inside the drum, while beating with the right hand. Effective, though brief, glissandos can be obtained by moving the left hand rapidly when the skin is struck.

Both fingers and flat of the hands are used for playing this instrument. A characteristic effect is the dead, 'slappy' sound obtained by the flat hand with a non-rebounding stroke. At the same time this stroke can produce different tones, for as the flat of the hand strikes nearer and nearer the rim, higher tones can be elicited.

The Arabic tabla does not equal the Indian one in its tone. In fact, its sound is comparatively thin and lacking in resonance. However, with its possibilities of pitch and tone modulation, it merits the attention of composers.

Boobams

Small bongo-type drums are fitted with long tuned resonators and fastened together in order of pitch, so as to form an instrument suitable for melodic use. The tone is hollow, melodious and resonant and the instrument is suitable for rapid passages, preferably played by sorbo-headed beaters. No definite compass for boobams can be given at the moment, as they are not yet in commercial production.

The model used for the record at the end of this book had a 2-octave chromatic range from F a twelfth below middle C to the F above. Due to the predominance of overtones, however, the instrument does not seem to sound in such a bass register, but gives an illusion (like the guitar) of sounding much higher. The instrument in question had all drum-heads of the same width (about 5 in.), the pitch being determined to a large extent by the length of the resonators, some being almost 3 ft long. This makes for a very cumbersome instrument at least 8 ft wide, and the above 2-octave range will probably not be exceeded.

Because of its light, melodious tones, this instrument should blend well with other tuned percussion, as well as being ideal for quiet solo passages.

13 | *tuned chordophones*

PIANOFORTE. HARPSICHORD. CIMBALOM

Pianoforte

Modern scores, whether for large orchestra or for chamber ensembles, frequently include the piano. For many composers it is just as essential a component of orchestral sound as any other instrument. To describe all the orchestral functions of the piano, and the technique of writing for the instrument, would need a book in itself. But here our objective is much more limited. We are concerned only with those aspects of the piano which can be legitimately included within the realm of percussion instruments.

We must therefore put aside discussion of piano as a concerto instrument, as a solo instrument within the orchestra (as in Messiaen's *Oiseaux Exotiques*) or even of those cases where pianos are the main orchestral elements, as in Stravinsky's *Les Noces*. We must ignore too the role of the piano as a supporting instrument, doubling other instruments in linear contours, supporting harmonies, and so on. In such solo and supporting roles the piano has a very important part to play, but the reader is certain to be aware of this. The present observations will therefore be limited to the functions of the piano as a member of the percussion group.

These functions derive from the piano's two main characteristics—its timbre, and the 'impact and decline' nature of its sound structure. Needless to say, these two characteristics are inseparable, and the use of the piano as a percussion instrument is usually dictated by the combination of both qualities. But in many cases one or the other may be predominant.

For instance, in the following example from Milko Kelemen's *Équilibres* for two orchestras, the piano is used to give a cold, hard background atmosphere, which combines with the cymbal roll to produce an icy, metallic shimmer. The actual pitch of the piano notes has no significance. Its function is only to produce a cool timbre:

Ex. 156 ♩ = 84   Kelemen: *Équilibres*

Here in its atmospheric role the piano part is largely 'static'. But the instrument may be used to give both atmosphere and movement:

Ex. 157   Schoenberg: *Accompaniment to a Cinematographic Scene*

It is difficult to give a precise description of piano timbre, indeed there are many varied opinions as to what good piano tone should be. In solo playing we often hear or read of a performer producing a 'warm' tone. But as far as the orchestrator is concerned, particularly in a percussion role, piano timbre is never warm and glowing. It is cool and impersonal, with a kind of neutral hardness. The extreme registers produce the most defined timbre, the lower notes having a dark metallic quality and the upper register a hard, thin brilliance. This is why the upper and lower registers of the piano are most used to double other orchestral instruments. The lower notes are often used to give a powerful precision and metallic ring to the basses of the orchestra, while the upper register is exploited to reinforce the upper woodwind, and give their sounds a hard, shining edge. We are not concerned here with such melodic usages, though they form important sources of effect for the orchestrator. Yet it is difficult not to emphasize the wide use of the piano as a percussive orchestral bass, either alone or with other instruments. No other orchestral instrument can produce such an incisive impact sound in the bass region, or contribute such a brilliant metallic ring.

In its role as an orchestral percussion instrument, the piano is very frequently used to give impact to chords. Perhaps the best known example is the beginning of Stravinsky's *Symphony of Psalms*:

Ex. 158   Stravinsky: *Symphony of Psalms*

Here the two pianos dominate the whole orchestra, and from the beginning of the work, set that dynamic tone and impersonal anti-romantic atmosphere so typical of the entire symphony.

Bartók uses piano chords to point the dynamics in energetic orchestral passages, or to pick out soft orchestral harmonies with touches of light:

Ex. 159   Bartók: *Music for Strings, Percussion and Celesta*

Percussive piano chords may also be of a non-harmonic nature, deliberately avoiding the orchestral harmonies. When used loudly, such chords have a 'shock' effect which virtually belongs to the realm of untuned percussion:

Ex. 160   M. Kelemen: *Transfigurationen*

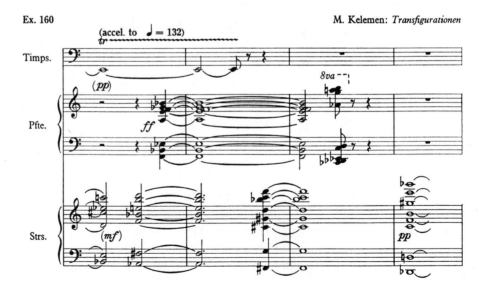

However, used in quiet passages, such non-harmonic chords produce a gentle obscuring of other harmonies which is subtle and attractive. The effect is not unlike that of a deep tamtam. In fact the combination of low piano chords and tamtams gives a wonderfully deep, mysterious sound:

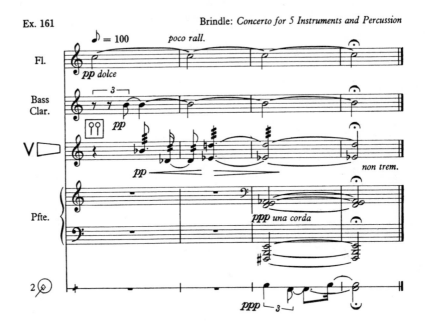

Ex. 161   Brindle: *Concerto for 5 Instruments and Percussion*

Note clusters are of excellent effect in 'percussion-piano' writing. In loud passages they serve to produce a formidable 'impact' sound as in the following example from Kelemen's *Transfigurationen*, in a passage of scurrying strings, stabbing woodwind, brass chords, and percussion tremolos:

Ex. 162   M. Kelemen: *Transfigurationen*

The upper clusters are played by the right forearm on white notes only while the lower clusters are played by the flat left hand on both black and white notes.

Quiet note clusters can produce a mysterious background atmosphere in the lower region of the instrument, which can serve either as a dark colour in itself, or as a means of obscuring the orchestral harmony. In the following example, Boulez uses tone clusters in the lower register of the piano as a dense background colour, in contrast to the voice and the accompaniment of other instruments, including the upper register of the piano itself:

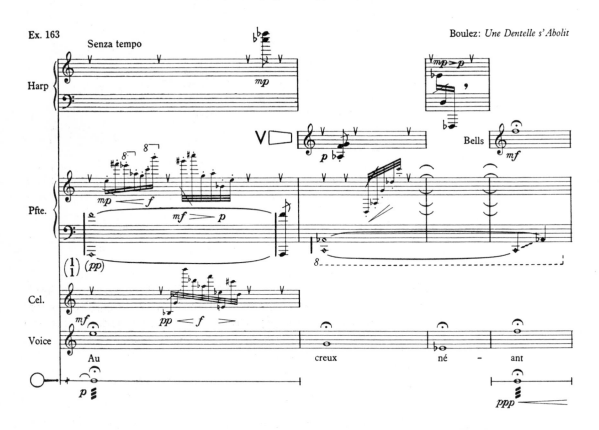

Ex. 163   Boulez: *Une Dentelle s'Abolit*

The first cluster is played by the left forearm on the white notes only, the second by the fingers of both hands in the normal manner. In the last bar the keys are released in turn from left to right to leave only the A flat sounding.

In aleatory compositions, the performance of tone clusters, glissandos, and 'fistfuls' of notes is often indicated by graphic symbols such as the following two sections from Haubenstock-Ramati's *Mobile for Shakespeare*:

Haubenstock-Ramati: *Mobile for Shakespeare*

Ex. 164

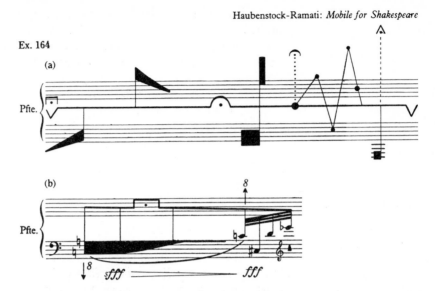

(a)

Pfte.

(b)

Pfte.

Naturally there is no exact interpretation of the above. Note clusters are the most obvious feature, both in vertical 'block' form after the central pause in (*a*), diminishing upwards in (b), and increasing upwards and diminishing downwards at the beginning of (*a*). Durations are in proportion to the graphic spacing.

Before moving on to discuss the less orthodox possibilities of the piano, it must be stressed that the instrument frequently joins company with other tuned percussion such as the xylophone, marimba, vibraphone, glockenspiel, and celesta. The piano has a natural ability to fit in with all these instruments in their normal functions. It can combine with them in percussive chords, running passages or background atmospheres (cf. the piano and celesta in the third movement of Bartók's *Music for Strings, Percussion and Celesta*), or it can provide a harmonic background to other tuned percussion.

In addition to normal piano usages, the instrument has also a wide range of less orthodox resources which are gradually entering into use both in chamber and orchestral music. Most of these unorthodox effects aim at bringing out colouristic possibilities of the piano which have never previously been exploited, and which offer a rich gamut of new sounds to the adventurous orchestrator. Many of these sounds have not a large scale of volume, and are perhaps more suited for use in chamber ensembles.

Pizzicato

The strings may be plucked either with the fingernails, or with the soft flesh at the finger ends. The nails produce a harsher sound and more volume, the finger ends give a softer tone. When the strings are plucked at their very ends with the nails, the timbre can be very thin and metallic. The bass strings can produce some powerful and varied effects, with a good body of sound. This effect may be indicated by the sign used in the example below, or by the abbreviation 'pizz.':

Ex. 165

Maderna: *Oboe Concerto*

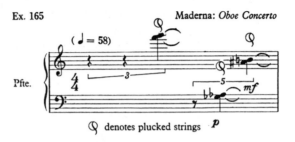

Ⓠ denotes plucked strings

The strings can also be plucked in groups with all the fingers of each hand, producing dense cluster sounds. In the following example the lozenge-shaped notes indicate the plucking of a number of strings in the registers indicated:

Ex. 166

Maderna: *Oboe Concerto*

molto sensibile e lasciar vib.

Naturally, with all pizzicato effects, the sustaining pedal must be depressed.

Harmonics

The piano is very rich in harmonic sounds, obtained by touching the strings lightly for a moment while the corresponding notes are played on the keyboard. Every string can produce a large number of harmonics, depending on the point where the string is touched. Harmonics at the octave, twelfth, and fifteenth are easy to obtain by touching strings at the centre, at one third of its length, or at one quarter of its length, respectively. The strings can be marked with chalk at the appropriate points, to help the performer find the harmonic 'nodes' with ease.

Harmonic sounds have a pure, firm tone, but only a limited scale of volume. Any attempt to force the volume will cause the sound to be marred initially by the impact sound of the hammer, so it is best to use this effect only in quiet passages.

Naturally, harmonics must be played singly, and the succession of sounds must be at such speed as to allow the player time to prepare each sound. The lower strings have the best effect, and naturally the low single strings are easiest to deal with.

To indicate harmonics, it is best to write the notes as struck on the keyboard and include the harmonic sounds in parentheses above, also giving exact information as to which harmonic is required:

Ex. 167

Harmonics produced while plucking the strings are also very attractive, with subtle shades of timbre, depending on whether the nails or soft finger-ends are used for pizzicato. Again, the scale of volume is rather limited if harshness is to be excluded.

Striking the strings

The strings of the piano can be struck with a variety of beaters, producing very different timbres. Timpani sticks, vibraphone, glockenspiel, or xylophone beaters, or even a metal triangle stick can be used. In general, soft beaters produce a mellow booming tone, and hard beaters a thin, metallic, clanging sound. With wide beaters, such as soft ball timpani sticks, it is difficult to sound single notes, but with small-headed beaters single notes can be played with ease, and the volume controlled effectively over a wide dynamic range.

The timbre can be quite unlike normal piano tone, the lowest strings can be made to clang like bells or boom out like majestic gongs. The upper region can produce sounds of brittle, glass-like texture. The colour spectrum depends not only on the type of beater used, but also on where the strings are struck. If strings are struck near the tuning pegs, harshness will result. Moving towards the centre of the strings, the tone becomes softer and less rich in harmonics. If the string is also touched with a finger at a certain harmonic node, this particular harmonic can be brought out with quite a striking timbre.

For striking the strings, two methods can be adopted. The sustaining pedal can be depressed (being raised when necessary) and the strings struck with beaters. It will be necessary to mark certain strings for identification purposes.

Alternatively, one hand can depress (silently) keys on the keyboard while the other is used to strike the strings. This method has three advantages. It avoids the sympathetic vibration of all the piano strings which occurs when the pedal is kept depressed (which may cause an unwanted jumble of sounds), and also the player can see which strings are to be struck, through the key mechanism raising the corresponding dampers. In addition, false notes are avoided, as only the undamped strings will sound. This permits a very soft wide-headed beater to be used. Unfortunately this method is not suitable for rapid successions of notes, for obvious reasons.

In the following example, both methods are shown, the first group of notes being played with keys silently depressed by the left hand, while the second group is played with beaters in both hands, and the sustaining pedal depressed. Square notes are used to indicate struck sounds; except for some aleatory indications such as that shown at the end of the following example:

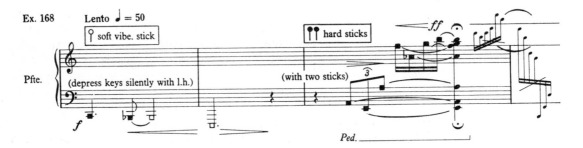

In addition, piano strings can be struck with the hands in various ways to give very varied and complex effects. Ingvar Lidholm has a prominent section featuring this in his orchestral *Poesis*, but in the concert hall it would seem that amplification is necessary for the full exploitation of these possibilities.

Muted piano

Unusual tone colours can be obtained by laying strips of cloth over the strings, or simply damping them with one hand while the other plays on the keyboard. Especially if pressure is used, this gives a dead sound with a rather clattering, percussive effect. Better results can be obtained by laying strips of plasticine 1 in. wide over the strings and pressing them down very slightly. Laid half-way along the strings they can produce a pleasant thin tone which is almost silvery in quality. They can be put in place and removed very quickly.

Wood or metal rulers laid over the strings will produce a distinctive metallic effect, especially if placed near the hammers. It is important to find the correct weight of ruler. If too light they will have little effect on the tone and soon dance out of place. If too heavy they will prevent vibration of the strings.

As the strings of the piano are usually divided into three or four sections by the metal frame strengtheners, it is possible to mute one section only, and leave the others for normal playing.

While the above muting methods modify the timbre considerably, the instrument can still be written for in a conventional keyboard manner, with all the usual running figurations, chords and so on. The most effective results are obtained with rapid arabesques, brief chords and note clusters which do not require sustained tone.

Stroking the strings

With the sustaining pedal depressed, the strings can be stroked with the fingers and fingernails, or with sticks varying in hardness from soft yarn vibraphone mallets to metal triangle beaters.

All kinds of glissando effects can be obtained on dynamic levels from pianissimo to fortissimo, with many different timbres. Wire brushes, or a few pieces of wire held in one hand, can produce quite complex sound patterns. Naturally it is essential to control these effects with the sustaining pedal.

Due to the normal division of the piano strings by the strengthening bars, it is best to indicate which area is effected. The effect, being somewhat aleatory, is best indicated by graphic signs which leave the performer to use his own invention within certain limits. For example:

Ex. 169

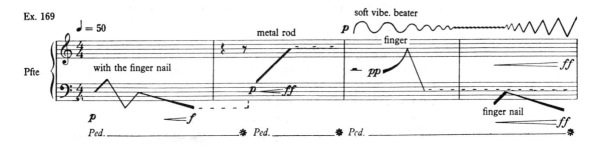

Scraping the strings

As the lower strings have a corrugated surface, being wound with copper wire, they can be scraped longitudinally with the fingernail or a piece of wood or metal. They can be scraped singly, or if a ruler is pulled over the strings towards the player, a fair number can be scraped together. Naturally the sustaining pedal must be depressed.

Various volumes of sound are possible, and the effect continued over any period. A very potent sound can be obtained with a big crescendo effect by drawing a ruler over the strings in a rapid sweep towards the player. Again, these effects can only be indicated by approximate graphic symbols:

Ex. 170

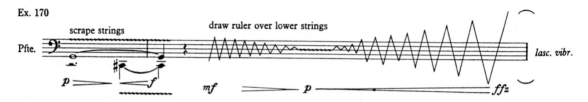

Note. For most of the unorthodox effects mentioned in the last pages the player has to stand up, lower the music stand, and otherwise prepare himself. He must accordingly be given time to do this, and also time afterwards to return to a normal mode of playing.

There are also several other percussive roles for the pianist, of a rather more banal character. For instance, in Maderna's Oboe Concerto the second piano player is instructed to play 'on the surface of the piano' with light sticks; in pieces by John Cage the player has to slam down the piano lid; while in Krenek's Flute Sonata there is a passage where the pianist plays on the cover with a metal coin. None of these effects is particularly ingenious or musical, and care must be taken to reserve such and similar usages for moments when they are apt. Otherwise, from an aesthetic point of view, the result can be catastrophic. However, a touch of humour is certainly welcome occasionally, and Cage manages to introduce entertaining moments of comedy into his works by means which other composers would never deign to use.

The Prepared Piano

Materials, acting as 'mutes', are placed between the strings of a piano with the object of changing the instrument's tone colour. Usually only a limited number of strings are so muted (e.g. eighteen notes in John Cage's *Amores,* fifteen in Toshiro Mayuzumi's *Pieces for Prepared Piano and Strings*).

The muting is done in various ways:

(1) Screws are placed between strings. As the upper half of the piano has three strings for each note, two screws can be used to mute all three strings. Alternatively, two adjacent strings can be muted with one screw and the third string left free to vibrate in the normal way.

The screws must fit fairly firmly between the strings so that there is a resonant sound, with no metallic buzz. A muted tone, rich in harmonics, should result.

(2) Metal bolts may be used for the lower strings, where a greater diameter is required to fit between the strings, and a heavier-gauge metal needed to impede their normal vibrations. The same type of sound should result as in the last section.

(3) Screws or bolts may be used as above, but loose washers or nuts can be inserted between the strings and the heads of the screws or bolts. When notes are played with this kind of muting, the loose washers or nuts will vibrate freely, rattling against the strings and impeding their vibrations, thus shortening the sounds, but producing a rattle or buzz.

(4) Strips of rubber 1 in. wide and $\frac{1}{8}$ in. thick are threaded under and over adjacent strings and pressed down firmly. The rubber strips are then pushed along the strings to the position of a harmonic node, so that when the key is depressed, harmonics will sound without the fundamental tone. The sound produced is dull, with a rather pronounced thud, but if suitable harmonic nodes are chosen, partial tones will sing out quietly with a pure timbre.

(5) Rubber wedges may be used instead of rubber strips for the lower strings where these are in pairs. The muting should result as in the previous section.

Regarding the preparation of a piano, John Cage, says 'the total desired result has been achieved if, on completion of the preparation, one may play the pertinent keys without sensing that he is playing a piano, or even a "prepared piano". An instrument having convincingly its own special characteristics, not even suggesting those of a piano, must be the result.' (Preface to *Amores*.)

The volume of the prepared piano is small, so it is not suitable for use with an orchestra. However, its sounds have a surprisingly quiet, whimsical charm all of their own, which would be valuable in chamber ensembles. Perhaps it may be added that for the author the prepared piano seems to have a faint oriental touch in its tones, but this may be a purely personal impression.

There is a practical consideration to be mentioned. It takes time to 'prepare' a piano and also to return it to its normal state. In addition, after being used as a prepared piano, the instrument is almost certain to need a small amount of re-tuning. It is therefore best to have two pianos available at a concert where prepared piano music is interspersed between normal pianoforte items.

Harpsichord

At present there is very little music which gives grounds for the supposition that the harpsichord may have latent potentialities as a percussion instrument. Since the baroque epoch, the harpsichord has been neglected, especially as an orchestral instrument, till such composers as Manuel de Falla and Frank

Martin reintroduced it in works of a concertante nature. But even in modern works the music is of a kind which seems to exclude any effects which can be legitimately claimed for the domain of percussion.

Nevertheless, there is no doubt that *in certain acoustic conditions*, the harpsicord could contribute colouristic and dynamic effects of a percussive nature. These effects are similar to the piano's percussion role—background atmosphere, percussive chords of a harmonic or non-harmonic nature, note clusters as impact effects or for obscuring harmonies, etc.

Unfortunately, it is the 'acoustic conditions' which pose the problem. For the harpsicord has such a tiny sound that in an instrumental ensemble it is inaudible in all but the most favourable circumstances. Its sound is apparently incisive and intense (in fact few instruments have such a brilliant yet grandiose timbre), but its volume is minimal.

Naturally, in radio transmissions such problems do not arise, and perhaps for concert performances the solution is to be found in amplification. Purists may cry out in horror, but there is no denying that with amplification, the harpsichord could prove a valuable source of colouristic and percussive effects, and could be used even with the largest orchestras. Indeed, it could very well prove superior to the piano in many percussive roles, due to its greater incisiveness and richness of timbre. At the time of writing, electronic harpsichords are appearing on the market. Most of them have a large dynamic scale, some being very potent indeed.

Modern harpsichords are made with a compass of five octaves, written:

There are two keyboards, each sounding strings of eight foot register (i.e. normal pitch), but of somewhat different tonal characteristics. The lower keyboard usually has also registers of sixteen foot and four foot pitch (sounding respectively one octave below and above normal pitch), and in addition may be coupled with the upper keyboard. The strings are plucked by leather or nylon quills.

The upper keyboard usually has a device for producing different tone on its eight foot strings. A mechanism is actuated to lower a strip of felt on to the strings, producing a short 'pizzicato' note, resembling lute tone. This device is termed the 'lute' or 'harp' stop, or sometimes simply 'sordina'. Occasionally the upper manual may have a four foot register, but this is by no means common and can be ignored for general purposes.

The various registers on each manual, the lute stop, and the coupling of manuals, are all brought into use by actuating foot pedals. *There is no sustain-*

ing pedal on harpsichords. Notes cease to sound as soon as the keys are released.

Unlike the hammer mechanism of the pianoforte, the quills of the harpsichord do not produce any dynamic graduations. No changes of volume can be achieved by striking the keys harder or softer. Dynamic alterations can only be obtained by adding to or reducing the number of registers in use.

It is usual to indicate the lower and upper keyboards as 'I' and 'II' respectively. The 'registration' (i.e. the registers to be used) must be clearly indicated at the beginning of the music, and also at each subsequent alteration. For example, beginning with sixteen foot and eight foot stops on the lower manual and an eight foot stop on the upper, changes of manual and registration may be indicated as follows:

| I. 16'. 8'. | - - - - | II ⎱ coupled
I ⎰ | - - - - | II. 8' lute | - - - - | I. 8'. 4'.
uncoupled |

Normally, changes of register are not made during a musical phrase, but between musical sections.

Cimbalom

The cimbalom or cimbalon is a type of dulcimer used in Hungarian 'gypsy' orchestras but seldom found elsewhere. It is similar to the piano (with multiple strings) but has no keyboard. The instrument is laid on a table or stand, the open strings running crossways before the player, the longer bass strings being nearest.

The instrument is played by striking the strings with special half-hook-shaped beaters. There is usually no damping mechanism, so the sounds ring on, together with all the harmonics they arouse on other strings. This makes the cimbalom most suited to music with running figurations, rather than to chordal progressions. Some modern instruments now have foot-operated dampers, but nevertheless, the typical role of the instrument is one of rapid arabesques and florid decorations. Until comparatively recently, instruments had a compass of only two or three octaves, but now they are usually made to range over four octaves from E below the bass stave to *e'''* above the treble stave. However, instruments may not be completely chromatic within this compass, for instance the low F is often omitted.

WHISTLES. SIREN. BULL ROARER. MOTOR HORNS

Whistles

Various kinds of whistles are used for realistic effects—police whistles, bird calls, train whistles, and so on. Even a large steam whistle has been included in one score. But fortunately such extravagances are none too common.

A slide whistle is sometimes used for playing melodies. This is usually a small metal vertical flute of cylindrical bore, fitted with an inner piston which can be moved up and down the tube, thus altering the pitch. The instrument has a sweet, pure sound, characterized by a prominent glissando when the piston is moved to obtain different notes. A gentle 'trembling' of the piston produces a vibrato effect.

In his ballet suite *Billy the Kid*, Aaron Copland introduces a brief melody with a 'tin whistle', played staccato. Presumably this is the tin whistle similar to the vertical flute with finger holes:

Ex. 171   Moderato ♩ = 100   Copland: *Billy the Kid*

stacc.

mp nonchalantly

In *Poesis*, Ingvar Lidholm introduces a bird whistle solo for a moment of light relief in the middle of this orchestral piece of fairly severe character. The result is quite comic, and produces a good laugh before the final cataclysm.

Siren

Sirens have been very little used in symphonic music. Hindemith used one in *Kammermusik* No. 1, as also Varèse in *Hyperprism* and *Ionisation*. All these pieces are absolute music and the instrument is not intended to be used in a realistic sense (as it is in Davidson's *Auto Accident*.) In his *Amériques* for large orchestra, Varèse uses the siren to a large extent, possibly to evoke the industrial atmosphere of North America. Unfortunately we are so accustomed to the siren sound for air raid warnings or police cars, that their use in the above pieces jars our aesthetic sensibility.

In *Ionisation*, Varèse writes for two sirens, high and low in pitch, operated by turning a handle, with a button for instantaneous braking—in fact he specifies the exact make and type. As the handle is turned faster, the pitch rises and the volume increases. In both *Hyperprism* and *Ionisation* the sirens are mostly sounded at low volume with slight crescendos and diminuendos, but at the peak points of the music they reach fortissimo and then are braked instantaneously.

Mouth sirens are sold by some firms. These are metal tubes with interior revolving perforated discs. They imitate the hand siren, but have considerably less power. They have been occasionally used, especially in jazz or popular music, for a comic effect.

Bull Roarer

A bull roarer or 'thunder stick' consists of a long, thin piece of wood, fastened to a piece of string. When it is whirled rapidly over the head, it produces a menacing, roaring noise.

That most enterprising of American orchestrators, Henry Cowell, used two 'thunder sticks' in a chamber work for string quartet, though this would hardly seem the right setting for such instruments.

Motor Horns

These are occasionally employed for either comic or realistic effect. In one score (Gershwin's *An American in Paris*) they are even given special tunings. Little comment is needed here, except to point out the two main categories—electric (diaphragm) horns and wind horns. These latter may be operated by a rubber bulb, and are usually played by circus seals! The exact mode of functioning of the new 'Continental' type motor horns is not clear (are they 'electric' or 'wind'?), but by their power and well defined pitch, they should certainly have possibilities.

THE PRINCIPAL ROLES OF PERCUSSION

1. PERCUSSION AS MELODY
2. PERCUSSION IN KLANGFARBENMELODIE
3. PERCUSSION AS HARMONY
4. PERCUSSION IN A HARMONY-OBSCURING ROLE
5. PERCUSSION AS COUNTERPOINT
6. PERCUSSION AS ORCHESTRAL COLOUR
7. PERCUSSION AS A FUSING FACTOR IN ORCHESTRATION
8. PERCUSSION AS DYNAMIC REINFORCEMENT
9. PERCUSSION OSTINATOS
10. PERCUSSION AS A FOURTH ORCHESTRAL DIMENSION
11. NATURAL SOUND EFFECTS
12. EXOTIC AND FOLK-LORE EFFECTS

Percussion can be rather dangerous. In some kinds of music it is quite out of place, in others it can be used with discretion. Elsewhere it may form the very core of the music. Percussion, if used at all, must be employed in a way which is completely apt to each particular musical situation.

This may seem obvious, but if we do not consider the exact role percussion should play in our music, the effect can be incongruous. Even the great can err. For example, one of Milhaud's later symphonies seems to be 'music without percussion' right up to the middle of the adagio. But here the lyrical expression is suddenly obliterated by a long passage for untuned percussion. Perhaps Milhaud only intended a contrast in mood. In reality he destroyed the spirit of his music.

No less important than deciding just how *much* percussion should be used, is the decision as to *what* instruments are most appropriate. Each instrument suits a particular atmosphere. It can add something to music of that same atmosphere, but elsewhere it can be catastrophic. For example, in Varèse's *Amériques*, sirens, anvils, and cymbals are perfectly in place in this picture of industrial America. But the work ends with temple block solos which evoke an exotic air quite out of keeping with the rest of the work.

It is therefore essential to decide at the outset whether percussion is suited to a work, and if so, which instruments are most in tune with its general atmosphere.

The Principal Roles of Percussion

The orchestral functions of percussion instruments are many and varied, and it would be confusing and tedious to deal with them all in detail. However, they can be arranged in fairly well-defined groups, and in the following pages these main functions are summarized in a general way. Obviously, the practical application of these principles must be left to the ingenuity of each composer or orchestrator. It would be wrong to give a catalogue of what should be done in every situation. This would only lead to a stereotyped practice which has nothing to do with living art. The art of music only lives through the constant renewal, by each of us, of a basic language which unfortunately in many aspects is already fairly threadbare. The percussion language is at present the least worn-out garment in the composer's wardrobe. Let us keep it so, by avoiding conventionalisms.

The following summary of percussion roles is therefore schematic and avoids discussion of particular applications:

1. *Percussion as Melody*

(a) *Solo melody*

The suitability of tuned idiophones and membranophones for solo melody has already been discussed as each individual instrument has been described. In brief:

Gongs, tubular bells, and timpani can range from sombre, dark moods to intense aggressiveness and thrilling triumph.

Crotales, celesta, and glockenspiel cover an expressive range from gentle, withdrawn moods to light, spirited expressions.

Marimba, vibraphone, and xylophone span the intermediary area between these two extremes.

Due to their inability to sustain sounds, none of these instruments is really suitable for sustained lyrical melody. However, the marimba and vibraphone can be to some extent, by using tremolo.

(b) *Doubling orchestral melodies*

Tuned percussion are used to double melodies played by other orchestral instruments:

(1) to add a percussive attack to the sounds
(2) to add a special timbre.

The addition of a percussive attack to a melody serves to add clarity and energy without a significant increase in volume. Even the most subdued melodic phrases can be given crisp outlines. Such phrases need not be leading melody, but can be background designs.

The timbre added by tuned percussion instruments naturally varies considerably according to the instrument used. The glockenspiel will contribute a shining aura, the xylophone a brittle surface texture, and so on. Obviously the timbre of the percussion instrument must match the tone of the non-percussion instrument. For example, the vibraphone goes well with the flute, xylophone with pizzicato strings, marimba with the clarinet, and so on. Doublings may be at the octave above or below, as well as at the unison.

2. Percussion in 'Klangfarbenmelodie'

This refers to that 'melody of tone colours' initiated by Schoenberg, and now such a feature of contemporary music. Schoenberg affirmed that sounds have two main dimensions, pitch and timbre, and that if melodies can be made with the pitch dimension, they can equally well be made with the 'other dimension'—tone colour. Time has proved him to be right in this supposition, for though a melody of timbres is not the same as a melody of pitches, it is nevertheless an expressive medium of some potency.

Percussion instruments are a valuable resource in *Klangfarbenmelodie*, for the range of their colour spectrum far exceeds that of other orchestral instruments. In this kind of 'melody', untuned percussion instruments are just as useful as those of definite pitch, for it is the timbre which is important, not precision of intonation.

Naturally, in *Klangfarbenmelodie*, percussion instruments can be used alone, or in alternation with other orchestral sounds, or to double other instruments. The following example shows a melody of timbres, first for percussion alone at 'a', and then alternating with other instruments at 'b'. In the latter section, percussion is used occasionally to double the sounds of other instruments:

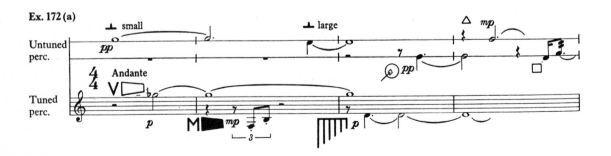

Ex. 172 (a)

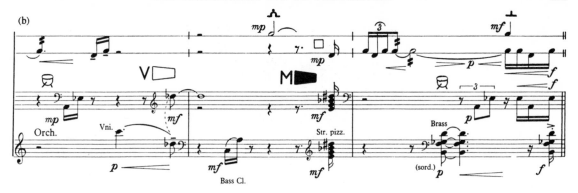

3. Percussion as Harmony

The role of tuned percussion instruments as orchestral harmony is fairly limited. The short duration of their sounds makes them suitable only in a few situations, while in this role they can soon become tiresome. However, they can occasionally have a refreshingly novel effect. Marimba and vibraphone are most suitable for middle harmonies, while glockenspiel and celesta can provide those evanescent chords which are so useful where fugitive harmonies are needed.

Perhaps one of the best means of providing harmony with tuned percussion is by sustained tremolo chords. The marimba and vibraphone are most suited to this role, as their tremolos are mellow and unobtrusive. This usage is most suitable for sustained internal harmonies in the low and middle registers (see Ex. 36).

Harmonies on a single tuned percussion instrument are too insubstantial for use with the full orchestra, so it is well to consider the use of a number of tuned percussion instruments together. For instance, chords on combined celesta, marimba, vibraphone, xylophone, piano, and timpani can form a full, vibrant sound with enough body to compete with other orchestral sections in mezzoforte.

As well as being used solo, tuned percussion can play a harmonic role by doubling other sustained orchestral chords. They give impact to the sounds and energize the harmonic movement, while the more conventional instruments function as sustaining factors.

4. Percussion in a Harmony-Obscuring Role

The evanescent nature of tuned percussion sounds makes these instruments invaluable when it is desired to obscure orchestral harmonies softly. The soft ringing tones of the vibraphone or celesta are most suited to this role. In the following example, these instruments cast a tenuous veil over the brass chord with sounds which are foreign to the harmony. But the effect of discord is minimal.

Ex. 173

Brindle: *Cosmos*

Untuned percussion such as cymbals and tamtams can be used for the same harmony-obscuring role, for they emit sounds which are almost certainly not part of any normal orchestral harmony.

5. *Percussion as Counterpoint*

Solo tuned percussion instruments are suitable for outlining a contrapuntal voice, especially in light orchestral textures:

Ex. 174   Dallapiccola: *Variations for Orchestra*

In heavier dynamic situations, they are naturally best doubled by some other orchestral instrument.

A number of tuned percussion instruments can be used in counterpoint, but the clarity of the horizontal flow of each part tends to be lost. A single tuned percussion instrument stands out clearly among other more conventional orchestral sounds, but when a number of tuned percussion play separate counterpoints, the situation is reversed. The horizontal flow of each part is obscured, and the result is an enigmatic interlacing of sounds.

However, this mingling of tuned percussion parts can be an asset in certain situations. The following example shows how tuned percussion and piano are first used to create a tangled rush of sounds which then unite in a violent splash of luminous colour, as if a wave of sound gathers up and breaks furiously:

Ex. 175

Brindle: *Homage to H. G. Wells*

This is an extreme case, where the tangling of parts has been deliberately cultivated to produce a result which no other orchestral instruments could create. But where clarity is an ideal, such complexity should be avoided.

6. *Percussion as Orchestral Colour*

For many composers, the timbre of a sound has assumed just as much importance as its pitch. Compositions have increasingly dispensed with the resources of melody, harmony, counterpoint and form in their more conventional guises, and inevitably other expressive means have had to be found to take their place. Timbre, as one of the most fruitful compositional factors which can be pressed into service to fill the lacuna left by the partial abstraction of the more conventional resources, has become one of the composer's main assets.

Percussion instruments, with their rich gamut of varied timbres, have therefore been a gift from the gods to many composers in search of colouristic novelty. Furthermore, most percussion sounds, even those of definite pitch, can be used without necessarily entering into those melodic or harmonic involvements which composers often wish to avoid.

This means that for many composers, the main function of percussion instruments has changed. Their role is no longer primarily dynamic, it is essentially and often exclusively colouristic.

The timbric resources of percussion can be used in two quite different ways, the one being the opposite of the other. In addition, these two usages can be combined, or superimposed one on the other. Timbre can be used (1) as a single basic colour over long periods, (2) as a succession of contrasting colours, or (3) these two usages can be combined—that is, a basic timbre can be used as a continuous background, and on this contrasting colours can be superimposed.

(a) *Timbre as Monocolour*

Musical sections, or even whole movements, often evoke a single atmosphere. This can be created by using one percussion timbre. There is no need to restrict this monocolouring function to one instrument only: the effect would be too monotonous. The right degree of variety can be obtained by using instruments within a specific timbre group. These groups are of course 'metals', 'woods', and 'membranes'.

For example, in his *War Requiem*, Britten uses percussion for monocolouring many sections. The 'Requiem Aeternam' has gongs and bells almost throughout, the 'Libera Me' is based on a constant background of drums, while the 'Sanctus' is formed over 'metal' tremolos. In his *Chronochromie*, Messiaen colours a number of sections entirely with xylophone and marimba, while others have a continuous substratum of bells and gongs.

An entire symphonic piece may be monocoloured with one class of percussion sound. For example, Messiaen uses metals throughout his *Et Expecto Resurrectionem Mortuorum*. Nono's *A Floresta* has a 'continuum' of sounds produced by bronze sheets, played both live and through the medium of previously recorded tapes. Naturally, a wide variety of timbres is created in order to avoid monotony, but the general colour-type in both these works is always metallic.

The use of a single type of timbre throughout a movement or extended section not only creates a constant atmosphere, it serves also as a unifying force, binding the music into one homogeneous whole. It is like the foundation colour to a painting which sets the picture's basic tone, but also unites all the separate masses and details.

(b) Timbre as Colour Contrast

Naturally, not all music is based on constant atmospheres. On the other hand, the very essence of many pieces is rapidly contrasting moods—contrasts which can be vivid and dramatic. It is here that percussion, with its wide colour spectrum, can play a telling role.

Where strong colour contrasts are needed, it is rather important to preserve the element of surprise. If a violent cymbal crash is needed at a decisive moment, the effect will be negative if the cymbal has been crashing away not long before. Paradoxically enough, the more vivid percussion colours must be, the less they should be used.

Inevitably, where timbres must be well contrasted, sounds from all three percussion groups—metals, woods and membranes—must alternate. Where less contrast is needed, instruments in the same group can be used. Naturally, this means that a study must be made of similarities and contrasts between the instruments of each particular group. For instance, taking the metal group, the triangle, glockenspiel and crotales are fairly similar in colour, but the triangle, cymbals and tubular bells contrast with each other. With the wood group, the wood block, claves, and high xylophone all have the same bright, 'chippy' timbre, but the castanets, temple blocks and low marimba each have quite different tones.

The relationship of percussion timbres to the colour of other instruments must also be considered. Similarities and contrasts are vitally important, but as a knowledge of these can only be gained by personal experience, it is not wise to list them here. This would only encourage a mechanical approach to orchestration.

Timbre contrasts as applied in *Klangfarbenmelodie* are also relevant here, but have been discussed in the previous pages.

(c) The Superimposition of Colour Contrasts on a Basic Timbre

One basic percussion colour can span a musical section, while contrasting percussion sounds are made to overlay this foundation. Naturally, some variety can be given to the basic timbre.

This method can give potent results of some complexity, and certainly provides a richer and more subtle play of colours than either (*a*) or (*b*) alone. For instance, a background colour can be formed by timpani and tomtom rolls (with variations in pitch and volume), and this mobile base can be overlaid with contrasting timbres from the wood and metal groups, sounds which can be sparse or dense as the moment demands. Such an effect—produced by only two performers, if need be—can give a very powerful and varied expression.

7. *Percussion as a Fusing Factor in Orchestration*
Percussion instruments have a magic power of making one kind of orchestral expression merge smoothly into another. We all know the kind of situation where the orchestra works up to a feverish climax, underpinned by a loud timpani roll. The orchestra breaks off. But the roll continues, dies down to pianissimo, and the strings at last murmur their way into an ecstatic andante. Such effects are commonplace enough. But it is important to recognize that without the fusing power of the timpani roll, the feverish climax and the ecstatic andante could not exist side by side. The result would be catastrophic.

This is rather a crude and banal example. But it serves to show how percussion sounds can merge quite contrasting orchestral expressions. Of course, the percussion instruments used in this role must be those whose sounds have some degree of continuity. Some instruments have to be rolled, but others may have sufficiently sustained sounds (e.g. tamtams, cymbals, etc.), so that rolls can be eliminated. (See Ex. 78.) If, however, the 'fusing' has to be done by a crescendo (to join a piano section to a forte), rolls are obviously necessary.

It is perhaps useful to indicate a subtle way of fusing by decrescendo. It is often possible for a percussion instrument to be struck at a lower dynamic level than the orchestral forte, so that it is not heard till the orchestra breaks off. Then its sound 'comes through' in a subtle way, and as the volume of sound fades, the next section can begin. This effect is only possible with metal idiophones.

This fusing function of percussion can be very effectively used in pointilliste music, or in any music where notes are relatively sparse and widely separated. In such situations, percussion can provide continuity of sound, and give unity and completeness to music which would otherwise be quite disjointed.

8. *Percussion as Dynamic Reinforcement*
The traditional role of percussion as a generator of dynamic accentuation is too well known to need much comment. In symphonic music, dynamic reinforcement by percussion is used mostly to underline the accentuations of the orchestra, or to build up the body of sound. Though these two functions often go together, it is important to recognize that this need not always be so. It is

possible to reinforce accentuations without adding much to the volume, and conversely, percussion can add significantly to the orchestral volume without producing any accentuation whatsoever (e.g. cymbal or drum rolls).

Today, dynamic reinforcement by percussion is often coupled with colour contrasts. For example, in the following short excerpt, four percussion instruments are used not only to strengthen the spasmodic accents, but to add appropriate flashes of colour:

Ex. 176

Dallapiccola: *Variations for Orchestra*

9. Percussion Ostinatos

Persistently repeated figures can form the foundation to a movement, giving it character and unity. Both tuned and untuned percussion are highly suited to this role, and if the ostinato is given a particular type of timbre, this can create a constant basic colour which sets the mood for the whole movement.

Usually an ostinato has a clearly defined rhythmic shape. To serve its purpose it should be simple, easily recognized, but not too obtrusive. If it is too complex, this will run counter to its efficiency.

The following example shows a short, concise ostinato figure for three tom-toms and three timpani:

Ex. 177

When ostinatos are simply sculptured, this allows music of a more complex nature to be laid over them without loss of clarity. It is also possible to super-impose yet another percussion ostinato figure over the basic one, to give a rich background without creating confusion:

Ex. 178

Brindle: *Creation Epic*

(The marimba, bongos, and tomtom are played by the same player in $\frac{5}{8}$ time at a different tempo to that of the rest of the orchestra. Note also the use of timpani as untuned percussion in this and the previous example. Their notes have no pitch significance and are heard only as low, medium, and high drum sounds.)

Contrary to the clarity aimed at in the last two examples, a number of relatively simple ostinatos can be used together to create a complex sound result, which is ideally suited to certain forms of expression. The three movements of Alan Hovhaness's Seventh Symphony are each based on ostinatos (drums in the first two movements; glockenspiel, vibraphone, and tubular bells in the finale) which are designed to give a complex background which is dense and enigmatic. The following example shows the ostinato designs for three drum players and timpanist which begin the first movement:

Ex. 179   Hovhaness: *Symphony No. 7*

As the movement progresses, these rhythms are always played in different combinations, so that the sound patterns are constantly changing.

10. *Percussion as a Fourth Orchestral Dimension*

The roles of percussion so far discussed have to some extent been secondary ones, they have been mostly in support of the other three main orchestral groups—strings, woodwind, and brass.

However, percussion instruments have become such a powerful and rich means of expression that they are beginning to be used in symphonic music as an ensemble, functioning as an orchestral group on equal terms with strings, woodwind, and brass. As a group, they no longer have a secondary role, but form a fourth orchestral dimension which has just as much expressive potentialities as the other three.

Furthermore, it is a dimension of unusual richness and variety. For the percussion ensemble can be sub-divided into a number of sub-groups, each with a different potential—metals, woods and membranes, each either tuned or of indefinite pitch: that is, six sub-groups which can each be used alone or in various combinations.

Neither the string, woodwind, nor brass groups have such varied resources. Yet not so long ago any orchestral composition which used anything more than a conventional minimum of percussion was regarded as freakish and hardly to be taken seriously. The truth is that the main mass of percussion instruments has entered late into the realm of music, and there has been some resistance to their invasion of the sacred territory of other instruments. However, large percussion sections are becoming more and more common, and there is little doubt that in the future this fourth dimension will have a permanent place.

The role of group percussion is similar to that of the other three orchestral groups—to function either as a body alone, to contrast with or oppose other groups, or to merge with them in the many complex ways which make up changing orchestral textures. Of course, the percussion group will rarely be used in its entirety. This would only produce a confusing conglomeration of different types of percussion sounds. It is more likely that the percussion sub-groups will normally be kept separate, so that their different sound characteristics may be kept pure and well-defined.

For instance, in the example on pp. 192–3, two different percussion sub-groups (tuned metals with piano, and membrane instruments) are used separately first in opposition to the orchestral tutti and then to full brass.

Naturally it is also possible to overlay one type of percussion timbre with another. For instance, a background timbre of untuned metals could be used as a continuous stratum of colour throughout a musical period, and on this, percussion sounds of other sub-groups could be superimposed, playing music of a 'foreground' type, equal in importance to the role played by strings, woodwind and brass. In other words, while one group of percussion plays a secondary role, the others can be made to overlay this with primary roles.

11. Natural Sound Effects

A number of instruments imitating natural sounds are available (e.g. cuckoo calls, cricket chirpers, bird whistles, train whistles, etc.), and these are used for unambiguously realistic sound effects. Others, such as anvils, cow bells, whips, and sleighbells, can be used for realistic purposes, but are mostly employed in symphonic music in such a way as to disassociate their sounds from naturalism.

Only a few natural sound effects have been mentioned in this book, because they do not normally play a legitimate role in concert music. Those which have been catalogued are in fact those instruments which are mostly used in a non-naturalistic way. However, a number of unusual 'natural' sounds do

Ex. 180   Brindle: *Homage to H. G. Wells*

occur in symphonic scores, for example, scores sometimes contain instructions such as 'break glass', 'drop coin', 'motor horn', and so on.

The truth is that the number of natural sounds which have been, and could be used, is infinite, and there is little point in cataloguing them today when tomorrow they may be superseded. Every composer is free to use whatever means he believes to be legitimate, and if he decides to use realistic effects of the most outré nature, nobody can protest as long as the aesthetic result is satisfactory. After all, when Rossini instructed the second violins to tap their music stands in *Il Signor Bruschino* he risked the sneers of the bigots, but how many smiles has he won with this genial touch?

12. *Exotic and Folk-lore Effects*

Some percussion instruments are closely identified with certain regions or peoples. They may have been cultivated exclusively by a certain race, so that their sounds still evoke suggestions of their origins. Though in most cases these regional instruments are used in concert music in such a way that their sounds have no suggestion whatsoever of local colour, it is nevertheless true that in the right circumstances they can be the most powerful means of evoking atmospheres associated with the lands where they originated.

Works for percussion ensemble are not very numerous, so no 'tradition' has yet been formed. The following few remarks can therefore be no more than advice of a general nature, based on such practical issues as have so far emerged.

The tonal resources of percussion are very varied, yet there is a danger that they may not be efficiently exploited. Works which use the various timbre possibilities of percussion continuously or haphazardly, will only sound confused, and from a tone-colour point of view, monotonous. For excessive colour variety produces monotony, just as much as does too little change of timbre. For instance, Edgar Varèse's *Ionisation* is not completely successful from a colouristic point of view, because despite the use of a large number of instruments, no clear colour contrasts are exploited. Most of the instruments play most of the time. Cage's *Construction in Metal* also seems to lack colour contrast, not only because of the exclusive use of metals, but also through too much insistence on certain instruments.

It is important to obtain 'clean' tone colours over sufficiently large areas, rather than mixed ones. This means that the six main resources of percussion (metals, woods, and membranes, in both tuned and untuned form) should be used separately more frequently than in combination.

Sometimes these colour contrasts are very simple indeed, usually conforming with the formal pattern of the music. Carlos Chávez adopted a very simple plan in his Toccata for six percussion players. In the first movement, only drums are used. In the second, tuned percussion (glockenspiel, xylophone and tubular bells) are laid over a foundation of untuned metals (cymbal and gongs) as in Ex. 66. In the third movement, there is a return to drums, with the inclusion of a few Latin American instruments in a minor role.

In this work, there is therefore a very clear relationship between timbre and form, perhaps excessively so, though as the work is not over-long, there is little risk of monotony in tone colours.

However, if pure tone-colours are used as successive blocks of timbre, there is an obvious danger of excessive sectionalization. The music will not flow, and will lack continuity. It is therefore important to elide colour sections skilfully, or to merge one colour into another. In the author's *Auriga* for four percussionists, the music is in one continuous movement, falling into six colour sections as follows:

1. Metals ⎧ untuned instruments
2. Woods ⎨ interspersed with tuned,
3. Membranes ⎩ in each colour.
4. Tuned percussion (metals and woods)
5. Mixed instruments (untuned)
6. Tuned percussion with untuned metals.

But these sections are merged, introducing instruments of the following section before the previous one ends. For instance, the first section includes tuned and untuned metals, but before it is complete, the castanets are already producing a background tremolo as a preparation for wood instruments.

Sometimes successions of colour are rapid and intense. In Jean Barraqué's *Chant Après Chant* there are colour changes almost bar by bar, but efforts have obviously been made to keep colours clear and unmixed. (See Ex. 181.)

Obviously these colour contrasts have been facilitated by using alternating groups of players. In the first bar, players I, III, and VI play woods (moku-bios, i.e., large temple blocks). These are immediately followed by membranes played by the remaining three players. In the fifth bar, players I, III, and IV introduce the mellow boom of the tablas, but again the remaining players interrupt, this time with metals (cymbals and tuned gong). Finally, there is a maximum mixing of colours. While three performers play on tuned woods and metals, the remainder sound untuned percussion of every type.

When timbre contrasts follow each other so rapidly, there is a danger that colouristic resources will be rapidly exhausted. In fact, this is what happens to some extent in *Chant Après Chant*, for once Barraqué has exploited the main colour contrasts, he falls into a general pattern of colour mixtures over long periods.

However, while we are intent on exploiting the valuable colouristic resources of percussion instruments, we must not ignore other assets they possess. On examining the scores of so many modern pieces for percussion ensemble, it is remarkable not only how the *melodic* resources of tuned percussion are neglected, but how their *harmonic* possibilities are quite ignored. With the sustained tones now available from tuned percussion (with or without tremolos), it is obvious that they can produce harmonic progressions just as convincingly as any other orchestral medium. Yet just because we are used to regarding percussive sounds as being of short duration, we are apt to assume that they are unsuitable as a medium for harmonic passages. We forget that the piano itself is a percussion instrument.

There are a number of practical matters which must be mentioned. Small percussion ensembles of up to six players usually have to rehearse without a conductor, so the task of preparing a work is greatly facilitated if all the players can play from a full score. The music should be written in large notation, so that it can be seen from a distance, so large pages are essential.

The score should be as simple and orthodox in notation as possible. It would greatly help percussion ensembles if all pieces were written in the same notation. Unfortunately, at the moment this is not so. It seems that every composer of a piece for percussion ensemble is determined to introduce a completely new notational system, so much so that in preparing works for performance, one member of an ensemble often has to dedicate himself to learning the notation and deciding how the music can be interpreted, before the piece can be tried out in rehearsal. Composers should remember that (as one member of an ensemble put it) any notation which is too difficult to read will never be played.

It is of great assistance to players if a plan of the percussion layout can be provided. Otherwise the ensemble has to waste some time finding which disposition of instruments fits the scoring.

One of the chief complaints of ensemble players is that composers seldom consider what sticks are most suited to a given passage. Often, indeed, no one type of stick is suitable. For example in Ex. 181 (Barraqué's *Chant Après Chant*) there are two points in particular where the correct sticks cannot be used. In the last two bars, the first percussionist has to play marimba, crotales, and mokubios together in the same phrase. Mokubios will only respond (with their slow-speaking, heavy tones) to soft, heavy beaters. These would be suitable for the marimba, but quite useless for the crotales, which need a light, hard beater. In the same two bars, the fifth percussionist has to play snare and tenor drums, gong, and cow bells in rapid succession. If the gong is meant to sound with its normal mellow boom, a heavy, soft beater must be used, while the drums and cowbells need hard beaters.

In these cases, performers have two alternatives. They can use beaters which are suitable for most of the sounds and ignore what happens to the others, or they can compromise, and use beaters which are mid-way between the contrasting needs of the various instruments. In the first case, some instruments will sound right, others wrong. In the second, there is the danger that all instruments may sound moderately well, but not well enough. In either event, the composer will be disappointed.

The only way to avoid such disappointments is not to take the easy path of leaving the choice of sticks to the performer, but to think out carefully every move the player has to make, decide on the exact nature of the sounds required, and exactly what beaters will be needed—in other words, the composer should put himself in the place of the performer, and write accordingly. This is the only true road to perfection.

Finally, in writing for percussion ensembles, it is important that the composer decides beforehand which type of ensemble he is going to write for. Ensembles are of two opposing types. In one, a large number of players is used, each playing a small number of instruments (as in Varèse's *Ionisation*). In the other, a small number of players is used, each playing a large number of instruments.

Works requiring a large number of players may be those designed for amateur performances (schools, colleges, etc.). Alternatively the composer may need a large body of performers because he wishes to build up a big mass of sound, with complex part-writing, even though only a few instruments are used. Compositions for a small number of players have usually a more virtuoso character, and a more limited volume of sound.

In any event, the number of players used is obviously governed by the colouristic variety required, and the difficulties in performance which must be solved. However, it must be remembered that percussion works have a certain 'theatrical' character, and it is much more interesting to see players in action, using a variety of instruments, than to watch them waiting their turn to play a single instrument. There is nothing less theatrical than a long line of percussionists counting rests!

17 | conclusion

Finally, in scoring for percussion, let us lay the myth once and for all that the percussion player is the imbecile of the orchestra. At one time he may have been a dull fellow, far below the musical standards of other players. But could any sensitive musician have been able to face the tedium of classical percussion parts year after year? Of course not.

Today, many percussionists are the keenest players in the orchestra. Given the slightest chance to show their skill, they will work like Trojans. The author's experience has always been that while most orchestral players disappear like mist in a wind during any rehearsal break, the percussionists will not only keep hard at work, but are anxious to clear up a pile of problems with the conductor or composer, and make suggestions for improvements.

Virtuosity must be provoked. It will only develop through being constantly challenged. The jazz drummer's virtuosity developed because it was demanded, while the classical percussionist's technique stagnated because nothing was required of him.

Jazz drummers have responded superbly in a situation which has allowed each individual's potentialities to develop fully. They may not all be able to read music well (they don't always need to!), but their manual dexterity and imaginative invention are often astonishing. For instance, the hand independence required for the following jazz solo is something most symphonic players would not care to cope with very often:

Ex. 182   Joe Morello: *Sounds of the Loop*

Fast tempo

(l.h. plays 2 Tom toms and Snare drum: r.h. plays ride Cymbal).

Naturally, in our scoring, it is wisest to keep within the bounds of what is reasonably possible. It would be foolhardy to write in a way which is beyond the skill of the average player (unless the music is written for a performer whose capabilities are already known). Nothing sounds well unless it is played well, and nothing sounds so awful as percussion which is not played well enough.

Yet though we must temper our enthusiasm and write with what moderation we can muster, we must still provoke players towards virtuosity, and present them with musical situations which encourage imagination and enterprise. We already know how jazz drummers have risen to the challenge. There is no doubt that symphonic players can respond just as well once their sense of adventure is roused—in fact their capabilities are increasing by leaps and bounds each year. Whoever a decade ago would have believed the following passage to be feasible?

Ex. 183

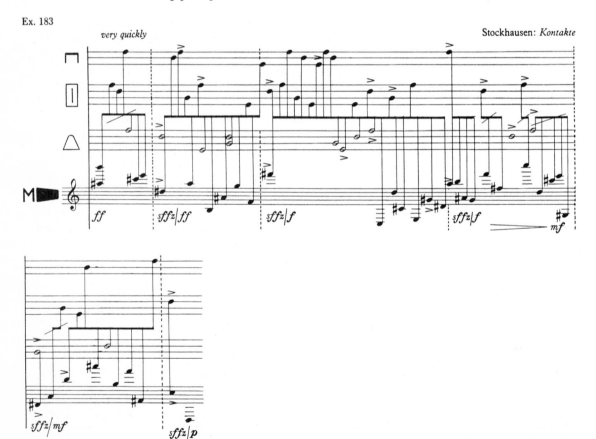

Such music needs as much virtuosity as any in the whole history of music. Yet several players have already overcome its difficulties.

One last word—there is another myth to be killed. In the past, percussion instruments were regarded as the 'noise-makers' of the orchestra. Unfortunately, some modern compositions seem intent on perpetuating this tradition. If, as is to be hoped, we are keen on eradicating this stigma, we must ourselves use restraint. We must underscore percussion, rather than overscore. We must learn the value of a few precious sounds, and eliminate the sound and fury that says nothing.

As one percussion player says: '*Bastano poche cose. Per l'amore di Dio, evitare il baccano !*'—'A few things (sounds) are enough. For the love of God avoid a racket!'

bibliography

Historical

BLADES, J.　　　　'The Orchestral Instruments of Percussion' in *Musical Instruments through the Ages*, edited by A. Baines, London 1961.
Percussion Instruments and their History, London 1970.

GALPIN, F. W.　　*The Music of the Sumerians and their Immediate Successors, the Babylonians and Assyrians*, London 1937.
Old English Instruments of Music, London 1952.

IZIKOWITS, K. G.　*Musical and Other Sound-Instruments of the South American Indians*, Göteborg 1927.

KIRBY, P. R.　　　*The Musical Instruments of the Native Races of South Africa*, Oxford/London 1934.

MARCEL-DUBOIS, C. *Les Instruments de Musique de l'Inde Ancienne*, Paris 1941.

MARTI, S.　　　　*Instrumentos Musicales Precortesianos*, Mexico 1955.

MAQUET, J. N.　　*Note sur les Instruments de Musique Congolais*, Brussels 1956.

SACHS, C.　　　　*Die Musikinstrumente Indiens und Indonesiens*, Berlin 1915.
The History of Musical Instruments, New York 1940.
The Rise of Music in the Ancient World, East and West, New York 1943.
The Wellsprings of Music, The Hague 1961.

SCHAEFFNER, A.　*Origine des Instruments de Musique*, Paris 1936.

SCHNEIDER, M.　　'Primitive Music' in the *New Oxford History of Music*, Vol. I, edited by Egon Wellesz, London 1957.

STAUDER, W.　　　A history of percussion instruments in *Die Musik in Geschichte und Gegenwart*, Kassel 1966.

WACHSMANN, K. P. 'The Primitive Musical Instruments' in *Musical Instruments through the Ages*, edited by A. Baines, London 1961.

Technique

ADAIR, Y.　　　　*Music Through the Percussion Band*, London 1957.

ABRAMS, M.　　　*Modern Techniques for the Progressive Drummer*, London 1965.

BLADES, J.　　　　*Orchestral Percussion Technique*, London 1961.

BUONOMO, A. and A. *L'Arte della Percussione, I–III*, Milan 1965. (With records illustrating instruments.)

CASKEL, C.	Modern percussion instruments and techniques in *Die Musik in Geschichte und Gegenwart*, Kassel 1966.
GOLDBERG, M.	*Modern School for Xylophone, Marimba, Vibraphone*, New York 1950.
KIRBY, P. R.	*The Kettle-drums*, London 1930.
KRAUS, P.	*Modern Mallet Method I–III*, New York 1958.
LUDWIG DRUM CO.	*The Ludwig Drummer, Chicago* 1961 ff.
PARNELL, J.	*Drums I–II*, London 1955.
ROBBINS, H.	*Modern Tutor for Xylophone and Vibraphone*, London.
SHIVAS, A.	*The Art and Science of the Timpani*, London 1964.
STRELSIN, W.	*New Method of Velocity*, New York 1954.
TORREBRUNO, L.	*Metodo per Vibrafono*, Milan 1957.
	Il Timpano, Milan 1954.
	Metodo per Strumenti a Percussione, Milan 1960.
WHITE, C. L.	*Drums through the Ages*, Los Angeles 1960.

Latin American

GSCHWENDTNER, H.	*Latin American Method*, Cologne 1958.
MARRERO, I. E.	*Drumming the Latin-American Way*, New York 1949.
MORALES, H.	*Latin-American Rhythm Instruments*, New York 1949.

Acoustics

BARTHOLOMEW, W. T.	*Acoustics of Music*, New York 1942.
CULVER, C. A.	*Musical Acoustics*, New York, 1956.
FOURNIER, I. E.	*L'Acoustique Musicale*, Paris 1953.
HELMHOLTZ, H. L. F.	*On the Sensations of Tone*, 1877. Re-issued New York 1954.
JEANS, SIR J.	*Science and Music*, Cambridge 1937.
LLOYD, L. S.	*Music and Sound*, Oxford 1937.
MILLER, D. C.	*The Science of Musical Sounds*, London 1916.
RICHARDSON, E. G.	*The Acoustics of Orchestral Instruments and the Organ*, London 1929.
STAUDER, W.	Notes on the acoustic properties of percussion instruments in *Die Musik in Geschichte und Gegenwart*, Kassel 1966.
TAYLOR, C. A.	*The Physics of Musical Sounds*, London 1965.
WALLER, M. D.	*Chladni Plates*, London 1960.
WOOD, A.	*The Physics of Music*, London 1947.

Orchestration

CASELLA, A.	*La Tecnica dell'Orchestra Contemporanea*, Milan 1950.
FORSYTH, C.	*Orchestration*, London 1914.
JACOBS, G.	*Orchestral Technique*, London 1931.
	The Elements of Orchestration, London 1962.
KENNAN, K.	*The Technique of Orchestration*, New York 1952.
PISTON, W.	*Orchestration*, London 1955.

nomenclature of percussion instruments in Italian, French, and German

English	Italian	French	German
Snare drum	Tamburo con corde	Caisse claire	Kleine Trommel
Tenor drum	Cassa rullante	Caisse roulante	Rührtrommel
Tomtom(-s)	Tom-tom(-s)	Tom-tom(-s)	Tom-tom (tomtoms)
Bongo(-s)	Bongo(-s)	Bongo(-s)	Bongo(-s)
Conga(-s)	Tumba(-s)	Conga(-s)	Conga(-s)
Timbale(-s)	Timpanetto(-i)	Creole(-s)	Timbale(-s)
Bass drum	Grancassa	Grosse Caisse	Grosse Trommel
Tambourine	Tamburello Tamburo basco	Tambour de Basque	Tamburin Schellentrommel
Timpano(-i)	Timpano(-i)	Timbale(-s)	Pauke(-n)
Xylophone	Xilofono	Xylophone	Xylophon
Marimba	Marimba	Marimba	Marimbaphon
Vibraphone	Vibrafono	Vibraphone	Vibraphon
Glockenspiel	Campanelli	Jeu de timbres Carillon	Glockenspiel
Celesta	Celesta	Celesta	Celesta
Tubular bells	Campane	Jeu de cloches	Glocken
Gong	Gong	Gong	Gong
Crotales	Crotali	Crotales	Crotales
Triangle	Triangolo	Triangle	Triangel
Cymbal(-s)	Piatto(-i)	Cymbale(-s)	Becken(-en)
Tamtam	Tamtam	Tamtam	Tamtam
Cowbell(-s)	Campanaccio(-i)	Cencerro(-s)	Cowbell(-s) Viehschelle(-n) Kuhglocke(-n)
Anvil	Incudine	Enclume	Amboss
Claves	Claves	Claves	Claves
Wood block(-s)	Cassettina(-e)	Bloc(-s) de bois	Wood block(-s) Holzblock (-blöcke)
Temple block(-s)	Block(-s) cinese	Temple block(-s)	Tempelblock (-blöcke)
Whip	Frusta	Fouet	Peitsche
Sistrum	Sistro	Sistre	Sistrum

English	Italian	French	German
Sleigh bells	Sonagli	Grélots	Schellen
Castanets	Nacchere	Castagnettes	Kastagnetten
	Castagnette		
Maracas	Maracas	Maracas	Maracas
Rattle	Raganella	Crécelle	Ratsche

index